The Dialogic Sign

Middlebury Studies in Russian Language and Literature

Thomas R. Beyer, Jr.
General Editor

Vol. 2

PETER LANG
New York • San Francisco • Bern
Frankfurt am Main • Paris • London

David K. Danow

The Dialogic Sign

Essays on the Major Novels of Dostoevsky

PETER LANG
New York • San Francisco • Bern
Frankfurt am Main • Paris • London

Library of Congress Cataloging-in-Publication Data

Danow, David K. (David Keevin),
    The dialogic sign : essays on the major novels of
Dostoevsky / David K. Danow.
        p. cm. — (Middlebury Studies in Russian language
and literature ; vol. 2)
        Includes bibliographical references and index.
        1. Dostoyevsky, Fyodor, 1821-1881—Technique.
2. Narration (Rhetoric).   I. Title.   II. Series.
PG3328.Z7T435   1991   891.73'.3—dc20   91-33847
ISBN 0-8204-1628-2   CIP
ISSN 0888-8752

The paper in this book meets the guidelines for permanence and durability
of the Committee on Production Guidelines for Book Longevity of the
Council on Library Resources.

© Peter Lang Publishing, Inc., New York 1991

Printed in the United States of America.

For Mirjana

Contents

Preface

All citations from Dostoevsky's novels are drawn from the original Russian texts. Page numbers in parentheses, following these passages, refer to the respective English versions listed under primary sources in the bibliography. Changes have been made in the translations where deemed necessary to conform more closely with the original. In several cases, passages have been cited which did not find their way into English in any form. Such instances, as well as others, are noted in brackets by a Latin numeral, signifying the volume, followed by the page number of the original Russian text.

Secondary sources included in the bibliography represent works that, for the most part, are directly cited in the text; a few selected studies that have implicitly contributed to the making of this book through a like critical vision are also listed. Quotations from secondary sources in Russian have been rendered into English throughout by the author. The transliteration system followed is that generally employed by Slavicists, except in the case of proper names, when more common usage applies, as in the case of the author of the novels that are the focus of this book.

1

Introduction

Narrative Models

The literary work attains a special status among the arts as a unique semiotic system. One set of relatively flexible rules, originating within a single encompassing genre that affords a work its guiding organizational principle, is embedded in another, stricter set composed of natural language, the basic material of verbal art. In the making of a work of literature, the literary canon, providing certain constraints, is thus accommodated by the linguistic code that makes demands of its own.

To that seemingly neat and simple schema, synoptic of the relation of language and literature, at least one qualification should be made. Specifically directed to the novel as genre, a certain reservation concerning the very existence of a governing "code" (or particular guiding format) can be attributed to the literary theoretician and philosopher of dialogue, Mikhail Bakhtin, whose theses have engendered many of the concerns and some of the findings of the present study. In his thought, the novel is conceived as boundless, as an ever-expanding and forever incomplete genre that is therefore understood to be largely unencumbered by canonical order. Hence its relative freedom from a delimiting generic rule. Preeminent among literary genres in its immanent design to counteract common rigidifying tendencies in literature, the novel, it is claimed by Bakhtin, knows little of the kinds of constraints imposed by other genres which, by virtue of their greater delimitation, more readily lend themselves to comprehensive definition.

The problem of defining the novel will occupy us here only so far as to acknowledge that, in the considered examination and exploration of any single novel, a firmer grasp results not only of the work at hand but of that seemingly elusive comprehensive definition aspiring (with little hope of succeeding) to encompass the entire genre. In seeking to define this relatively unencumbered narrative form, one can only strive to keep pace with certain representative instances that appear to exemplify the genre best. Yet those instances, paradoxically, frequently serve to extend its "bounds" in the process. Attempts to define the novel as genre thus respond more broadly to the task of elaborating a poetics of the novel. But since the novel form is forever incorporating within its domain new representative instances that uncompromisingly demand a corresponding revision of our understanding of the genre, perhaps all that can be said with assurance about the novel is that each is governed by its own individual poetics or set of organizing rules. Yet that understanding only acknowledges that each is unique.

Our aim at the outset of this study is therefore to outline a critical approach, oriented toward that particular configuration of aesthetically organized language that we commonly recognize (but may not be able to define) as the novel. Serving as a general point of departure, the concept of employing a literary model, conceived most basically as an ordered pattern of coherence, will be addressed in this opening chapter and then utilized concretely as a series of interrelated strategies in subsequent discussions of Dostoevsky's four major novels: *Crime and Punishment* (1866), *The Idiot* (1868), *The Possessed* (1872, more accurately translated—but less well known—as *The Devils*), and *The Brothers Karamazov* (1880). In treating these works from complementary perspectives, the purpose of this book is to contribute to an understanding of the highly distinctive poetics of the Dostoevsky novel. This means, in effect, to demonstrate what makes his writing *different* not only from his contemporaries but also within the global context of world literature.

As our point of departure, the concept of a literary model is understood to encompass a set of exemplifying schemata, ideally affording broad applicability. Designed to evoke the bounds by which a given subject is delimited, it may serve as a hermeneutic device in the analysis of verbal art. Affording a hypothetical framework within whose bounds a given subject is theoretically contained, a literary model is thus an ideal concept yielding a pattern of order, implicitly followed by the critic, much as the governance imposed by genre is adhered to by the writer. An aggregate of characteristic elements, encompassing its subject in concrete or figurative illustrative terms, its function is both descriptive and interpretive. It thus serves as a clarifying instance, comprising a certain abstract schema, whose aim is to project a corresponding set of determinate relations, intended to illustrate the principles by which a given subject might have been generated or may later be explicated.

As a comparatively primitive model, abstract definition may function as the cohesive force that secures and integrates the figurative and literal aspects of a given philosophical view, ensuring a unified and convincing argument in the process. As a critical case in point, the concept of dialogue, pivotal here in its concrete sense—but currently accruing various figurative encrustations of meaning as well—requires such formulation. For present purposes, to be elaborated further, dialogue is understood to encompass verbal and nonverbal modes of communication that are responsive either to previous or anticipated utterances, articulated by one or more speakers.[1]

A model may also be viewed as a kind of *example* designed to afford an inclusive "image" or likeness reflective of some other, more expansive idea, and is thus iconic in this regard.

Hence the Russian term for "model" (*obrazec*) exists in relation to the etymologically related term for "image" (*obraz*), where the former is clearly derived from the latter. The idea of a model is thus closely related to—in this particular linguistic instance, even derivable from—the notion of pictorial representation or some other kind of excmplification.

In its most general aspect, as an ideal construct, a model is designed fundamentally to set forth an abstract set of relations that can be said to apply between the given model and its subject. As a particular case in point, and as has long been known, interesting results obtain when the novel is taken as generic model, and its subject is perceived as the world. Subsumed within the general, in other words, is the specific case of the novel as model—the world of the novel as model of the actual world. As Yury Lotman affirms, "a work of art is a finite model of an infinite universe . . . a work of art is in principle a reflection of the infinite in the finite . . . " (1977:53). And, as Bakhtin declares, 'the concept of genre is "a mode for representing the world" (1981:28). Both thinkers make essentially the same point—that the literary work is designed to represent in aesthetic form a certain recognizable world. Regarding the novel in particular, the idea is concisely formulated thus: "The basic convention governing the novel is the expectation that readers will, through their contact with the text, be able to recognize a world which it produces or to which it refers . . . " (Culler 1975:192). Unmistakable in their lineaments, these views are clearly drawn from the veritable tradition that conceives of art as mimesis, as a vast, intricately related modeling system of the world.

From the standpoint of Bakhtin's now current notion of the chronotope, specifying the time/space coordinates of "any and every literary image," the elaborate temporal and spatial configurations that govern the perception of the actual world (as part of a given culturally engrained perspective) are those that determine as well the making of a text. As Bakhtin puts it: "Out of the chronotopes of our world (which serve as the source of representation) emerge the reflected and *created* chronotopes of the world represented in the work . . . " (1981:253). But the process also works in reverse, as both the world and the world of the work appropriate what they need from one another—in the fundamental human activity of making sense of the world through art—resulting in a series of potentially infinite progressions. This mutually influenced, dual-directed flow of information may be directly attributed to the merging of two interrelated normative systems: the cultural codes of the actual world with the literary codes that are superimposed upon the represented world in narrative. For it is the concatenation of these two distinctly related systems that affords the literary work its modeling capability in the first place.

A model's constitutive features ideally encompass the subject it is meant to elucidate. In analogous fashion, as meaningful fragment within a virtually infinite configuration of like artifacts, the text mirrors the greater context of which it is a part in necessarily truncated but potentially significant form. As the product of the artist, performing, in this related sense, a similar reflective function, the aesthetic text is the proper, and primary, generic analogue to an elucidative model—itself a complementary, but secondary, creative endeavor—produced by the analyst. The former, as cultural manifestation, is designed to reflect the world in some sense, while the latter, as critical device, is conceived, in turn, to mirror the text.

What would appear the most appropriate generic literary model is one that necessarily takes into account the fact of an author's individualized use of language as a fundamental constituent of verbal art. In seeking to produce a complementary work of literary analysis, the critic must strive to achieve a balance between the application of language-oriented models and a given writer's particular linguistic usage. Such approach would, ideally, grant the literary work its special status as a unique semiotic system, where the literary code is embedded within the proper norms of language—but where those norms are further subject to the particular vagaries of individual idiom.

Inherently disposed toward intrinsic modes of approach to the literary work, the point of view just outlined does not advocate one critical method over another but acknowledges the utility of a designated model as interpretive technique in the concrete endeavor of literary criticism. From this standpoint, the individual work of art, as a unique representative instance, is treated as such through the application of a descriptive model that implicitly recognizes the work's *sui generis* status as an original and unrepeatable language construct, governed by an individual poetics that at once partakes of the generic norm, while generating a superimposed code that is strictly its own.

*

In the chapters that follow several related and juxtaposed problems are treated. As the principal rubric of this study, dialogic relations are conceived as a mesh of interwoven verbal and nonverbal modes of communication, which afford, at times, striking primacy to the latter. In such instances, gestural activity emerges as the primary signifier, largely in the absence of speech. As the generally predominant mode, however, speech evokes a sense of immediacy that makes even the past seem present at the moment of its telling. This quality of fictional narrative may be partially accounted for by the frequent inclusion within dialogue of reported speech, representing past-oriented structures of discourse that are revitalized by their recapitulation in the present. In accord with the striking prominence attained by reported speech within the novels themselves, in this book the topic achieves a repeated like prominence—even when our ostensible concern is directed elsewhere.

A speaker's words are never quite laid to rest in Dostoevsky's novels. Instances of reported speech—ranging from Raskolnikov's and Ivan Karamazov's related views to Stavrogin's own conflicting theories—are repeatedly examined within their respective contexts. The critic can do no less. Reported speech, in effect, mirrors its own function; designed to resurrect a previously spoken word, it demands as well its own repeated resurrection as a rubric that is fundamental to the consideration of dialogic encounters from various interlocking perspectives. Moreover, the dialogues themselves— Raskolnikov's talks with Porfiry and with Sonya, Myshkin's with Rogozhin, Ivan's with his lackey and his devil—demand repeated consideration essentially for the same reason. Their dynamic intensity resists containment by a single analytic approach. Like reported speech, itself a fundamental component of dialogue, the extended discussions of the novels are also seen to overflow their purported bounds in an abundance of meaning that elicits further responsive reaction.

Nowhere in the Dostoevsky canon does reported speech figure so centrally as it does in *The Possessed*, where Stavrogin's past utterances represent the novel's ideological and political pivot, upon which the entire action of the novel turns. Yet nowhere in that novel does its central hero express his own ideas. Likewise, analogous to a pronounced absence of direct speech on the part of Stavrogin in *The Possessed*, we find a parallel absence of dramatized present *event* in *The Idiot*, resulting in a poetics of absence that focuses the discussion of Chapter Three. In both novels, moreover, there is a distinct absence of dialogue among the principal characters which, paradoxically—in a canon founded, as Bakhtin presumed, on principles of dialogue—extends to *The Brothers Karamazov* as well. This paradox will find its place in the course of our discussion. However, to anticipate, a typical strategy of the Dostoevsky novel is to establish a direct counterpoise between some of the most dynamically engaging dialogue in world literature and its sustained absence.

In *Crime and Punishment* and *The Brothers Karamazov*, Raskolnikov's and Ivan Karamazov's like "idea," whose basic similarity is commonly acknowledged, is also not articulated by its respective author. Their essentially jointly held theory affirms the individual's right to amoral conduct in the interest of accomplishing some "higher" aim. For Raskolnikov, the idea is rooted primarily in historical example; Ivan derives it from an inverted theological position. Yet in both Dostoevsky's first and last major novels, the fundamentally atheistic idea is expressed within analogous dialogic structures composed of reported speech and ironic discourse intended to discredit a theory, which is at the same time first being adumbrated. Characterized by a seeming paradox—the simultaneous articulation and rejection of an idea— such discourse is treated in Chapters Four and Five, devoted to the two novels, and to showing how the idea in both instances is ultimately devalued by essentially the same technique.

In neither novel is there a single occasion when the pivotal idea is articulated in impressive, convincing manner. In its dramatic realizations, it is consigned instead to such twin sorry manifestations as the murder of an avaricious old woman and a drunken sot of a father. Denigrated at the start of each work, it is displaced from the characters' discourse for long periods thereafter. As the guiding principle, however, generating in each novel its corresponding pivotal event—which is generically the same in each—the idea is transplanted, as it were, from the mind of its author (Raskolnikov, Ivan) to that of the reader, where it can neither be readily assimilated nor easily dismissed.

Within its respective dialectic, neither novel allows for a balanced, judicious presentation of its hero's governing thought. Instead, the idea is first presented unsympathetically as reported speech; it is then minimally defended by its author, in the case of Raskolnikov, and in no real sense at all by Ivan; and is finally reduced to ashes at the end—by Raskolnikov himself in the presence of Sonya, and in more abstruse fashion by Ivan's devil—which *is* Ivan—in the presence of Ivan. Raskolnikov can offer neither Sonya nor himself a convincing rationale whereby the means justify the ends, which is all the idea seeks to demonstrate in either case, as Ivan's devil readily proclaims. Ivan must also ultimately reject his own formulation, since (in both novels) the idea reduces to an elaborate justification of criminal self-assertion—which in Dostoevsky's world is always murder.

That fictive world is represented as an artificially constructed verbal universe composed of language in its multiform diversity. Our intent, in part, will be to explore a single delimited area within a rich domain of possibility: the use of reported speech to reinforce one viewpoint within dialogic structures generally expressing mutually opposed intentions. The confrontations between Raskolnikov's past and present selves and between Ivan's former and present egos allow for a single viewpoint to emerge as triumphant—that which contradicts what is simultaneously expressed. As reported speech, in these and other instances, the idea is interwoven with thoroughly conflicting intentions and intonations, producing internalized dialogue within a single speech utterance. No utterance among those considered, in other words, may be taken at face value, since each belongs to more than one speaker—or to the same character at different periods. The internally dialogized word, as Bakhtin terms it, is thus continually evident as an utterance saturated by mutually conflicting points of view struggling for a sympathetic hearing.[2]

The same such struggle for ideological predominance is evidenced thematically in *The Brothers* by a similarly dense, highly proliferated internal modeling system, composed of the many independent story forms of the text, whose composite effect is to produce a definitive structural complexity that distinguishes *The Brothers* from Dostoevsky's other novels. Effecting a "dialogic thematics," or complex arrangement and juxtaposition of the mosaic-like narrative components inherent in *The Brothers*, the internal modeling system immanent to that novel invites, in effect, a corresponding critical approach founded on an "external" set of models superimposed on those operating within the text itself. The extensive series of small narrative forms structuring *The Brothers* are thus treated in Chapter Five as iconic signs that mirror both plot and theme. Uniformly termed "subtexts," these story forms represent accounts that are either intimately connected with the characters of the novel and their personal histories or are more closely related to the novel's contending ideological concerns. In all instances, however, details of the subtext are shown to have their clear analogues within the greater text, whose ideational premises and dramatic turns, conversely, are refracted through the variegated prism of an internal modeling system that heightens their effect.

In Chapter Six, these same minimal story forms are viewed from a related standpoint as indexical signs that either anticipate or generate further events in the novel's necessary progression from beginning to end. Designed to take *The Brothers* from its opening in the past to its conclusion in a present that heralds the future, such concentrated narrative forms are crucial to the novel's thematic, compositional, and ideological concerns. Hence their potential importance, outlined thus: "The conflict between different ideological (evaluative) points of view often appears in such specific genres as the anecdote. The analysis of the anecdote on this level . . . may prove useful, inasmuch as it may be considered a relatively complex compositional structure. Consequently, it may be considered an analytically convenient model of the artistic work" (Uspensky 1970:11, fn.8). Our purpose in Chapters Five and Six, devoted to Dostoevsky's last novel, is to demonstrate in critical practice the evident virtue of that "analytically convenient model" purported in theory.

As another type of subtext, modes of nonverbal communication are treated in the following chapter as a complementary form of communication that is generally subordinate to the predominant verbal form. This varied mode nonetheless achieves formidable significance as a series of independent signs whose meaning is essentially context bound. Independent in the sense of being unintegrated within any codified system, such signs are nonetheless highly integrated within the novels' respective dialogic structures, whose dynamic quality may be accounted for in part by Dostoevsky's distinctive repeated recourse to nonverbal communication as a form that may wholly supplant the otherwise dominant verbal mode. It is commonly acknowledged, in the words of a Russian Formalist thinker, that "The significance of expression and gesture . . . is very great . . . Expression and gesture sometimes play the role of a reply in dialogue, replacing verbal expression" (Yakubinsky 1923:121-22). But with Dostoevsky, in particular, gesture as a means of communication attains "a level of importance that is equal to that of verbally expressed thought (*slovesno-zvucašče oformlennaja mysl'*), since the articulated reply exists, as it were, in the gesture itself and with the help of gesture" (Mikhailov 1972: 102). Gesture, in other words, may figure as importantly as, or even predominate over, speech. Evident in all of Dostoevsky's major novels, such singular effect is achieved within a series of subtly calculated shifts, realized through the repeated transposition of word and deed, whereby one communicative mode is transmuted into the other, as characters are periodically deprived of speech and thereby transformed into actors.

While the vast majority of scholarly efforts have been devoted to the character's word as signifier in dialogical interaction in fiction, manifestations of nonverbal communication in isolation from speech, as well as the integration of speech and gesture as joint signifiers, are clearly fundamental aspects of fictional dialogue. Most common are instances where speech is the predominant signifier, at times accompanied by gestural support. But a more dramatic instance of dialogic interaction emerges when a form of nonverbal communication appears as the primary mode—when expressive gestural activity is performed, essentially, in silence.

That is frequently the case in Dostoevsky. As one critic notes: "Naturally, in the work of other writers dialogue is linked with gesture, but if the center of gravity of their dialogue is contained in the objective logical meaning of the word (*predmetno-logičeskom značenii slova*), in Dostoevsky it is centered in the gesturally expressive (*žesto-vyrazitel'nom*)" (Ibid.:104). This mode of "gestural expressiveness" is particularly evident during Dostoevsky's "verbal tournaments," which are frequently initiated in silence and are later punctuated by further extended periods devoid of speech. At such moments, gestural (including facial) expression is noteworthy for being not simply the predominant but the *sole* signifier, contributing to the characteristic intensity of such "duels." This feature of Dostoevsky's art will be shown in the following chapter to be fully encompassed within a readily delimited model, concerned, in effect, with how an essentially dramatic technique is vitalized within narrative discourse.

The idea is neatly summed up in these succinct terms: "In Dostoevsky's dialogue the characters actively speak (*govorjat-dvižut'sja*) in words that are also gestures (*slovami-žestami*)" (Ilyushin 1969:24). Momentarily transformed into actors, Dostoevsky's animated speakers gesture their intended meanings. Interestingly, all of the hyphenated Russian expressions just cited are seemingly created ad hoc by their respective authors in a collective effort to communicate what is distinctive about dialogue in Dostoevsky. These particular formulations testify to the special, unique quality of an art that demands analogous creative expression as an appropriate critical response.

As a final instance of such intended response, the expression *"govorjaščij žest"* (Mikhailov 1972:103) neatly encapsulates the overall argument of the following chapter. Broadly rendered as "expressive gesture," it may also be translated as the "gesture that speaks." It is this latter, less elegant turn of phrase that more closely makes our point. In Dostoevsky, a character's gestures do not so much supplement what is said as "articulate" what cannot or should not be communicated in words.

2

Nonverbal Strategies

The Major Novels

Dialogue in a literary work encompasses two different orders of communication. First, as a convention of reading fiction, we allow that information is communicated between characters, who "speak" to one another. Second, as a result of the reading process, information is transmitted from the text to the reader. Through dialogue, as one means of transmission, information is directed to a recipient within the world of the novel and, by extension, to the reader who participates in that world. For the latter this is accomplished almost exclusively by verbal means, aided by punctuation and, at times, by typographical notation. (A series of suspension points, for instance, may be employed to indicate a pause or hesitation on the part of the speaker, which the reader will then interpret within the given context.) The message received by the reader is thus conveyed on the printed page bearing essentially a single sign system. But this is not the case for the character depicted on that page. For if we are to regard the novel as being in some sense a model of the world, we must grant that in contrast to the reader's situation, the characters are confronted by a plethora of signs and sign systems which they are obliged to interpret. The signifiers of their world, we are to assume, are as multifarious and complex as those of our own.

Within the characters' realm, there exists a recognizable world in which a certain drama unfolds in novelistic time. When engaged in dialogue, the character interprets not only the spoken word but the nuances of meaning conveyed by the speaker's gestures, actions, and expressions. Although it is part of the reader's task to interpret all this as well, such information is transmitted to him as descriptive narrative independent of the dialogue per se, while the fictional character, made actively to participate in a world of the author's making, perceives it directly as action. In Dostoevskian dialogue, characteristically, the immanence of action within what is essentially a speech activity contributes to make that dialogue dramatic and to cause the reader to perceive it as such.

When Dostoevsky's characters finally engage in talk (a crucial confrontation may be strategically delayed for half a book or more) dialogue and drama become synonymous, as the interlocutors converse in fear and trembling. When engaged in dialogue, they shudder, tremble, twitch, grimace, contort their features, laugh loudly and challengingly, or lapse into prolonged silence, while disappearing into the light or darkness of their own thoughts. All such bodily registers or changes in facial expression, here collectively termed "gesture,"[1] constitute signs requiring interpretation. Detailed descriptions of a character's features at a given moment in dialogue are clearly meant to signify. The proof of this (should one be needed) is that the characters themselves react with striking regularity to the nuances of meaning implied by an interlocutor's change of expression or sudden distracting preoccupation, by an odd pose or unusual posture, and regard these as gestures signifying something concealed and meaningful. The reader can do no less. Dostoevsky's characters regularly interpret the meaning of such signs, either by commenting upon them or responding directly as though to the spoken word. By its very repetition and general profusion, gesture in Dostoevsky's novels becomes a sign not only for the character engaged in dialogue but, ideally, for the reader as well.

A similar argument may be made for the moments of silence which punctuate Dostoevskian dialogue. A halt in speech followed by an ensuing period of silence cannot be viewed as simply a pause or break in the momentum already generated but as a moment of intense inner debate, when a character is engaged in taking the measure of his interlocutor (frequently an ideological opponent) or in taking stock of himself. Reflecting a consciousness in turmoil, the moment of silence is active rather than passive. Often pivotal in terms of the course the renewed dialogue will take, such moments are purposefully incorporated into the communicative act of dialogue, and thus require interpretation on the part of both interlocutor and reader. As an integrated feature within dialogue, the moment of silence bears information (however obscure) on some level of meaning. To consider otherwise, particularly when the characters (themselves the novelist's creations) do not, would mean effectively to diminish the text. Hence the need for interpretation arises legitimately and necessarily when one or both interlocutors have momentarily grown silent.

According to common consensus, dialogue implies the presence of intermeshing verbal material. The utterances of one speaker alternate with those of another. But this basic understanding does not adequately encompass either everyday usage or literary dialogue, since communication—in both the actual and fictional worlds—is also achieved nonverbally through various responsive manifestations of gestural activity. In order to explore just this activity in Dostoevskian dialogue, what is never uttered but only gestured at—perhaps eliciting a (verbal or nonverbal) response in return—will be of present concern. In short, the focus will be on the gaps, on the moments of communicative silence.

Nonverbal communication and the possible interaction between speech and gesture represent common fundamental aspects of fictional dialogue. Novelists regularly depict such interaction as fully integrated, complementary means of signification. A character's speech, in other words, is linked to and supported by immediately accompanying or simultaneously occurring gestural activity. While this common device is also employed in dialogue authored by Dostoevsky, a high degree of intensity and corresponding specificity is achieved and defined by his compelling use of verbal and nonverbal signs frequently *independently* of one another. Language and gesture function as separate but nonetheless complementary modes for generating meaning.[2] In surveying various modes of communication, Roman Jakobson observes that "manual gestures and facial movements function as signs supplementary to verbal utterances or as their substitutes" (1971:705). While this supplementary role is employed both by writers in fiction as well as by individuals in daily discourse, Jakobson's latter consideration—where gesture functions as an independent sign lacking a verbal counterpart or when gesture serves as substitute for the word—represents the more telling feature in Dostoevsky's art.

Since critical attention has generally been concentrated on verbal communication in Dostoevsky, the focus of this chapter will be directed at selected instances when the burden of meaning falls not on verbal interaction but on the highly charged moments of narrative time when speech is temporarily interrupted, although the continuum of communication is not. In concentrating upon nonverbal communication in literary dialogue, as opposed to the primary verbal mode, two interrelated oppositions must be considered: Speech as opposed to Silence, and Gesture in relation to Stillness.

Clearly, a speaker may gesticulate to convey information while speaking, or while maintaining silence. Conversely, one may remain still while either engaging in, or refraining from, speech. There is therefore the possibility for speech whether the character gesticulates or not; likewise, gestural activity may be accomplished in silence. That these oppositions are interrelated and interdependent is thus immediately shown; not a single feature from among these four possibilities can be logically effected entirely exclusive of the others. Speech or silence is inevitably accompanied either by some form of gesture or by the character remaining still. And the converse is also true; a character's gesture or stillness will be depicted in conjunction either with speech or silence. Further, as the single mode of verbal communication, speech may be contrasted with silence, gesture, or stillness as potential modes of nonverbal communication in both quotidian and literary dialogue.

Hence, in terms of dialogic interaction, there are four logical possibilities: speech accomplished in conjunction with gesture, silence accompanied by gesture, speech accomplished in the absence of gesture, silence effected in the absence of gesture. From this basic framework, or model, emerge the following attendant cases, representing the only possible interrelations between modes of verbal and nonverbal communication in dialogue.

1. Speech appears as the predominant semiotic system within dialogue, nullifying all other possible signs. In this instance, only a speaker's utterance is communicated to the reader with no additional descriptive information provided.

2. Silence emerges as the predominant sign, nullifying all other possible signifiers. In this case, only the fact that an interlocutor has grown silent is reported.

3. Gesture is accomplished in conjunction with speech. What is stated is conveyed to the reader along with a description of the speaker's accompanying gesture or facial expression.

4. Gesture is accomplished in conjunction with silence. The fact that a character gesticulates is communicated—along with the acknowledgement of an accompanying silence, which in itself represents an auxiliary signifier of related importance.

5. As a final possibility, stillness as a potentially communicative posture is maintained during a speech utterance, or in silence. Immobility as a particular stance on the part of a speaker is reported; however, such posture represents essentially a rare instance—that is rarer still when maintained in silence.

Yury Lotman suggests that what distinguishes gesture from language or "any communication system employing signs which are ordered in a particular manner" is that gesture is "completely or almost completely unordered" (1977:8-9). His argument might well be extended to include silence as an additional component of dialogue and as a sign belonging to no ordered system. Although neither is codified, both silence and gesture (the latter when accompanied by speech and, more conspicuously, when not) function dramatically as signs within Dostoevskian dialogue. What makes us resist unqualified agreement with Lotman, therefore, is the fact that, in extensive counterpoise to Lotman's stated theoretical view, Dostoevsky has consistently endowed his characters engaged in dialogue (although generally one to a greater degree than another) with the ability to interpret not only verbal utterances but gesture as well, as though it were also a highly formalized (that is, codified) system of communication.[3] His characters consistently react to what is never uttered but only gestured with an utterance of their own, perhaps accompanied by a further responsive gesture. The Dostoevskian character never asks what is meant by an interlocutor's gesture or silence; rather, the character always seems to know,[4] and is thus granted the ability not only to interpret verbal utterances but also to comprehend the gaps. This distinctive feature argues, paradoxically, for nonverbal modes being coded on some level in the novels of Dostoevsky—if not for the reader, then surely for the character, who interprets them accurately and consistently. As Bakhtin explains it: "A deep essential bond or partial coincidence between the borrowed words of one hero and the internal and secret discourse of another hero—this is the indispensable element in all Dostoevsky's crucial dialogues . . . " (1984:254-55). Thus acknowledged, this "indispensable" feature merits greater attention than its mere mention.

In semiotic terms, two interlocutors are made privy to or share the same (secret) code. This evident comprehension of an additional code to that of natural language provides for a dual feature which, among others, makes Dostoevskian dialogue dynamic in the sense that there is always signification and communication, even when not a single word is uttered. Hence there are no real pauses or rest periods, but rather what Lotman refers to as "the semantic significance of pause, the measurement of the information carried by artistic silence" (1977:51): that high pitch of intensity maintained by the characters'—and reader's—straining for meaning and understanding.

To exemplify this and much of the preceding, let us cite a single illustrative passage from *Crime and Punishment*. Raskolnikov, the novel's protagonist and murderer of an old pawnbroker, responds with vexation, as well as concern for his mother and sister, when unavoidably confronted by his only friend Razumikhin.

> "Once for all, never ask me about anything. I cannot answer you . . . Don't come to see me. I may perhaps come here . . . Leave me, but . . . *don't leave them*. Do you understand?"
> It was dark in the corridor; they were standing near a lamp. For almost a minute they looked at one another in silence. Razumikhin remembered that minute all the rest of his life. With every moment Raskolnikov's intent and fiery glance pierced more powerfully into his mind and soul. Suddenly Razumikhin shuddered. Something strange had passed between them . . . some idea, something like a hint, something terrible and

> monstrous, suddenly understood on both sides . . .
> Razumikhin grew pale as a corpse.
> "Do you understand now?" said Raskolnikov abruptly,
> with painfully distorted features . . . (301)

Raskolnikov poses what might appear to be essentially the same question twice. Yet repetition does not produce identity; nearly a minute of silence has elapsed, yielding a new and different context. The significance of this time lapse is acknowledged when the query is repeated: "Do you understand now?" In the interval Razumikhin shudders, indicating by this slight gesture an emotional upheaval, as he finally comprehends that his friend is a murderer. Raskolnikov's face in turn becomes painfully distorted now that his secret has become known. The burdensome communication is accomplished without either uttering a word.

"Something strange had passed between them . . . some idea, something like a hint . . . suddenly understood on both sides . . . " These authorial words are emblematic of the kind of nonverbal or gestural signification which is an inherent, definitive feature of Dostoevskian dialogue. To demonstrate the immanence of this mode, the following extended dialogues within the major novels will be discussed solely from this single viewpoint: the meeting between Stavrogin and Tikhon (*The Possessed*); the several talks between Myshkin and Rogozhin (*The Idiot*); the three discussions between Raskolnikov and Porfiry, and between Raskolnikov and Sonya (*Crime and Punishment*); the three interviews between Ivan and Smerdyakov (*The Brothers Karamazov*).

*

"At Tikhon's," the famous expurgated chapter in *The Possessed*, depicts the only encounter between Stavrogin, the novel's spiritually bankrupt protagonist, and the strange unorthodox monk, Tikhon.

Shortly after starting out for the meeting at the monastery, Stavrogin abruptly stops on the way to check his inner pocket, smiles, and continues on his way. The first of these two gestures suggests that he is ascertaining whether something is in his possession, but what that may be remains to be learned. Likewise, whether the smile is genuine, ironic, or sinister is also unclear. If the reader were to reflect upon these gestures later, in the light of new information, it would be evident that both are related to Stavrogin's plan to publish his "confession." He checks his pocket to assure himself that the document is at hand, and smiles at the thought of the sensation it will make. At their first mention, however, what these gestures might signify remains a mystery inspiring a modicum of interest and curiosity. The reader is left to wonder what is hidden away there to evoke the strange smile.

Initially, a vast array of puzzling information is provided regarding Stavrogin's chosen confidant and shy interlocutor, as a further means of evoking curiosity and interest. It is stated that the other monks treat Tikhon with no great respect, and there are numerous hints suggesting unseemly behavior. He is variously charged with drunkenness and insanity, with having a multitude of feminine admirers, with careless living and even heresy. The fact that the reader is advised that such disparaging innuendos are not to be credited only enhances their intrigue. Other strange revelations follow, including the report that among the singularly unusual furnishings in his cell are a number of elegant gifts. Gold and silver icons are placed only a short distance from engravings "of a worldly nature," while the shelves are lined with spiritual writings alongside theatrical compositions and "perhaps much worse." The cell's furnishings are thus semiotic or information bearing, which contributes to their owner's enigmatic portrait, and makes plausible his later mundane, "aesthetic" interpretation of Stavrogin's confession. To round out further the peculiar portrait, Stavrogin enters the cell to find the monk occupied with war maps, and is immediately convinced that he is quite drunk. Such, then, is this recluse, who is extraordinarily disposed to secular affairs, and to whom Stavrogin intends to reveal his own lower depths.

Their encounter likewise begins in no ordinary fashion; their incipient dialogue is initiated in silence, as the guest enters and immediately becomes lost in thought. Tikhon at first appears peculiarly ashamed, with eyes lowered and an inane smile playing on his features. Yet, suddenly and unexpectedly, he fixes the other with an intent look, eliciting a slight tremor from his silent interlocutor as a kind of "response."

> The quiet waked him, and it suddenly seemed to him as if Tikhon were sheepishly lowering his eyes and smiling a completely needless smile. This instantly aroused a feeling of disgust and rebellion in him; he wanted to get up and go out . . . But [Tikhon] suddenly raised his eyes and looked at him so strongly and so thoughtfully, and at the same time with such an unexpected and enigmatic expression that he almost winced . . . (700)

Thus, with spare gestures amidst a tense silence, the meeting between sinner and cleric begins, in which the latter eventually proclaims his intent to make his crime of assaulting a young girl known to the world. Yet, strangely, from the very beginning it seems to Stavrogin that the monk has already anticipated his intentions. And this disturbing realization initiates their talk, as Stavrogin finally confronts his specially chosen interlocutor directly.

> "And you knew for certain that I brought something with me?"
> "I . . . guessed it from your face," Tikhon whispered, lowering his eyes.
> Nikolai Vsevolodovich was rather pale, his hands trembled a little. For several seconds he stared, motionless and silent . . . (706)

In this short passage are evident all four previously juxtaposed elements of verbal and nonverbal communication (speech and silence, gesture and immobility), functioning here as signifiers within dialogue. Moreover, it is during these moments of intense (internal) debate, when Stavrogin remains both silent and motionless, that he determines to reveal the mysterious document, which he then hands over to Tikhon.

That one of the participants in the drama may be possessed of special insight is characteristic of Dostoevskian dialogue. Premonition on the part of an interlocutor plays an important role in the confrontations between characters, and attains to the level of a convention which the reader is obliged to accept as a condition in reading Dostoevsky. That condition is grounded in a character type endowed with peculiar characteristic traits, which are polarized in an odd capacity for appearing physically unprepossessing, foolish, and insecure, coupled with a remarkable facility for making highly perceptive observations.

Tikhon's insights ("I . . . guessed it from your face")[5] are generally accompanied by a characteristic lowering of the eyes. Throughout the meeting, in fact, he appears ashamed of what he "knows"—that is, of what he perceives and understands beyond what he is told. At one point, Stavrogin remarks critically upon Tikhon's typical expression: "You just now lowered your eyes again. . . . And, you know, that doesn't at all become you" (703). Ironically, Stavrogin himself later makes the same telling gesture when asked if it might be easier for him if he were to be forgiven. "'Easier,' Stavrogin answered in a low voice, lowering his eyes" (728). Stavrogin's overall discomfort, however, is generally depicted through the repeated mention of his ironic smile accompanied by continually trembling hands, and in bursts of nervous laughter followed by repeated lapses into thoughtful silence, engendered in each instance by constant irritation and the recognition of an incongruous situation which he himself has initiated. Finally, the perspicacious monk perceives what is concealed behind the other's enigmatic gestures. In a fictive world governed by an artistic vision which affirms that a crime is always committed as much against oneself as against another, Tikhon declares: "I see . . . I see as if in broad daylight . . . that you, poor lost young man, have never stood so close to a new and even more violent crime than right this minute!" (734). The crime which Tikhon foresees is Stavrogin's impending suicide. For Tikhon to "see" means for Stavrogin to be seen through; his stated intention to publish the document is perceived as only a delaying device at best against a far more serious intent. An integral part of the fabric of Dostoevskian dialogue, insight is transmuted into foresight—a transformation that represents a shift from psychological penetration to thematic prefiguration.

Having read Stavrogin's confession, Tikhon comments upon it in aesthetic rather than moral terms: "'The ugliness will kill it,' Tikhon whispered, lowering his eyes." Moreover, he is certain Stavrogin will be unable to bear the public ridicule his project is sure to engender. Such candid evaluation in turn inspires Stavrogin's uncertain question: "And you think I won't endure it?"—to which Tikhon's response is silence. Stavrogin interprets that silence as affirmation of his own assertion: "You know people, and you think that I in particular won't be able to endure it" (731). But Tihkon's mute reply also implies a further realization: that the document represents a challenge, rather than an act of repentance.

> "But you seem to hate and scorn beforehand all who
> will read what is set forth here and to be challenging
> them to a fight . . . "
> "Me? Challenging them to a fight." (725)
> Tikhon was silent. [XI,24][6]

Again Tikhon responds by remaining silent—a sure sign that he remains firm in his view.

That both interlocutors are silent for extended periods during their meeting is made evident throughout. Aside from the hour long period during which Tikhon reads Stavrogin's confession (and consequently there is no talk), the reader is repeatedly informed of the tension in the cell, where frequently the only response is silence.

> Tikhon held his tongue. (700)
>
> The silence lasted a long time, about two minutes. (700)
>
> Stavrogin stopped talking and suddenly fell again into his old thoughtfulness . . . already for the third time. . . . More than a minute went by. (705)

After Tikhon has finished reading the document, and Stavrogin probes him for a response, intermittent lapses into silence become an even more prominent feature of their intense dialogue. This becomes evident in the course of only two consecutive pages, during which their talk becomes increasingly strained, as the moments of silence become more frequent and burdensome.

> Tikhon quickly lowered his eyes. (725)
>
> Tikhon was silent. [XI,24]
>
> Tikhon was silent once more. Stavrogin . . . again fell into deep thought for moments on end. [XI,25]
>
> Again silence. (727)

Both interlocutors lapse into silence at numerous intervals throughout their encounter, as each tries either to interpret the other's unwillingness to speak or to recoup his seemingly

lost position. Meanwhile each displays certain repeated gestures that require interpretation: Stavrogin's ironic laughter
and trembling extremities, Tikhon's constantly lowered gaze
and insecure smile. At various moments within their talk, the
semantic weight is borne alternately by a moment of silence, a
gesture, or word. The latter is predominant; yet the former two
dialogic features constitute a consistently employed device,
designed to communicate telling information. Stavrogin's
silence ("Nikolai Vsevolodovich was silent") and gesture ("His
eyes lit up; he folded his hands together suppliantly . . . He
burst into laughter distractedly" 733-34) convey his spiritual
turmoil, which Tikhon clearly perceives, but whose eventual
course he cannot avert. Although he is endowed with a special
gift of understanding, the monk's own sense of helplessness is
made manifest by his very silence and continually lowered gaze.

Typical of Dostoevskian dialogue in general, speech and
gesture during this meeting are frequently depicted as independent communicative modes—but with one nonetheless supporting and confirming the meaning of the other. Stavrogin's
displeasure at Tikhon's continued exhortation (that he not
publicize his crime) is thus registered on two planes: first,
gesturally (through authorial mention)—"A sickly expression
was reflected on Nikolai Vsevolodovich's face"—then, verbally
(through Stavrogin's direct speech)—"and in general all our
explanations are beginning to be unbearable" (733). Both
modes contribute to the overall effect, and express essentially
the same thing; in this instance, that Stavrogin will shortly put
a halt to the whole proceeding, and go on to perform his final
act of self-abnegation. Not simply a descriptive element but an
integrated part of the entire dialogue, what is "reflected" on
the features of the one speaker is of real consequence for the
other as well as for the reader. What affords Dostoevskian
dialogue its specificity and characteristic intensity is, then, the
author's use of both silence and gesture as related devices for
heightening the tension produced by the characters' speech,

into which these two modes are integrated as formidable signifiers of another order both concluding and conclusive, the importance of gesture within the dialogue at hand is thematically underscored by the very fact that it is solely a gesture which tortures Stavrogin, and causes him actively to conjure into memory the image of the little girl helplessly threatening with an outstretched fist.

> But what is unendurable for me is this one image, precisely on the threshold, with its upraised and threatening little fist, only the way she looked then, only that one minute then, only this shaking of her head. That is what I cannot bear, because since then I have seen it in my mind almost every day. It does not come into my mind by itself, but I call it up, and cannot help calling it up, although I cannot live with it. (722)

Hence the power and expressiveness of a single gesture, within this artistic vision, for the character made to witness it and for the reader upon whose memory it also becomes engrained.

*

The intent of this chapter, necessarily delimited in scope, is to offer a perspective from which Dostoevskian dialogue may be construed as a "generic" structure embracing prominent nonverbal features in addition to speech. From this standpoint, the task at hand is to demonstrate that such diverse instances as the single meeting between unorthodox monk and depraved nobleman, and the several talks between an idiot prince and a mad bourgeois are structurally linked by a network of similar patterns, or by the employment of essentially the same definitive techniques.

Like Tikhon's cell—with its odd combination of the secular and the clerical, which bears directly on the peculiar monk who resides there—Rogozhin's house casts dark shadows on its gloomy inhabitant, and is even more a part of the large design. As in the previous instance, the setting and its occupant stand in a certain relationship to one another. Representing in oblique fashion an extension of its owner, Rogozhin's house fulfills the same semiotic function as Tikhon's cell. "The house is somehow inhospitable and frigid; it seems to be keeping something dark and hidden . . . " Along with merchants and *skoptsy*,[7] strange secrets are harbored in the place, and these have a bearing on Rogozhin himself. Thus the prince is able upon first visit to recognize it from afar: "That must be the very house!" (197). In that single statement, two conventions of the Dostoevsky novel intersect. First, there is frequently a semiotic connection between a character and the structure he inhabits; second, a character—particularly one engaged in the novels' extended dialogues—may possess the special, intuitive insight that Myshkin exhibits.

Myshkin's initial visit to that house is unexpected and ill-considered, as is made evident by Rogozhin's obvious displeasure.

> Seeing Myshkin, he turned so pale and was so petrified that for a time he stood like a statue, gazing with fixed and frightened eyes and twisting his mouth into a strange smile of utter bewilderment, as though he felt the prince's visit something incredible and almost miraculous. (198)

As in Tikhon's cell, the dialogue here, too, begins nonverbally, with the language of gesture (interpreted for the reader in the above passage's final phrase) taking primacy over speech. Rogozhin's frozen stance and stony immobile features are so expressive they cause Myshkin in turn to be taken aback, prompting an immediate response in the unexpected guest: "perhaps I've come at the wrong moment? I can go away, you know" (198). But Myshkin is invited to enter, as Rogozhin accepts what he considers to be a challenge. For a few moments longer, however, the wordless encounter continues as the prince indiscreetly scrutinizes his host in an attempt to probe the latter's discomfort.

> Not sitting down but standing motionless, he looked Rogozhin straight in the eyes for some time; at the first moment they seemed to gleam more brightly. At last Rogozhin smiled, though still rather disconcerted and somehow lost. (198)

Only when Rogozhin finally comments on his guest's fixed gaze ("Why do you stare so?") is the spell of silence broken. Initially, then, the incipient dialogue gravitates around a gesture (Myshkin's ungracious examination of his host) and silence. In this instance, the relation between the nonverbal and verbal components of Dostoevskian dialogue is wholly typified. First, gesture generates speech; the latter produces either further verbal communication, new gestural activity, or silence— itself a communicative feature that requires interpretation, and therefore once again generates speech, or more dialogue in its dominant mode.

To suggest that the ensuing dialogue between Myshkin and Rogozhin is composed solely of their alternating speech implies a too limited description of a structure infused with other dynamics at work—all contributing to a general intensification of the communicative act. Rather, their talk is composed of independent gesture as well and the responses it elicits. Upon arriving in Petersburg, to cite a striking example, Myshkin had felt a pair of eyes upon him in the crowd at the railway station. Later, he mentions this (somewhat abruptly and too directly) to Rogozhin who appears to shudder upon hearing the prince's words. ("As I got out of the train this morning, I saw a pair of eyes that looked at me just as you did just now from behind.") Rogozhin's slight shudder is enough to suggest that those piercing eyes in the crowd may very well have been his, although he appears to deny it ("You don't say so! Whose eyes

were they? . . . Well, perhaps it was your fancy; I don't know."
199). Since no other character in the novel possesses such a
pair, they belong either to him or to an unknown—which is
highly unlikely. When Rogozhin smiles a moment after
Myshkin's observation, this may also be interpreted as sly
affirmation regarding the penetrating eyes in the crowd. In
Dostoevskian dialogue a smile is always expressive—yet rarely
of mirth. In this case, however, the question is to be resolved
no further than by a shudder and a smile, since these two
dialogical features are more revealing (or expressive of the
truth) than Rogozhin's verbal response.

Rogozhin's penetrating eyes, flashing at key moments ("and
his eyes kindled" 205), represent only a single characteristic
feature, among others, which allow him to speak in the language of expressive gesture. His laughter is always forced and
irritable ("Rogozhin laughed but gave no explanation. . . .
Rogozhin laughed malignantly. . . . Rogozhin laughed, as he
listened to Myshkin." 352,354); his face is frequently distorted
or grimacing ("and his face worked with spiteful mockery" 206),
as he emits a sound ("Ha,ha! . . . Ha! . . . Ha-ha!" 206,208,
209,etc.) that signals a change of mood or disorientation in an
unbalanced mind. His constant vexation and sense of impotence
are revealed in those mirthless, powerful exhalations of laughter which leave him tired and frustrated. So rich and expressive
are the characteristic gestures endowed him, it would seem
they alone are sufficient in revealing his passionate, tortured
being.

Briefly noted, the following related instances further demonstrate the significance of nonverbal communication as a
wholly integrated feature of these tortured talks.

When Myshkin admits to Rogozhin that he could never be
a rival, he immediately registers the latter's reaction: "Now you
are laughing. I know what you are laughing at." Clearly, Myshkin has interpreted the gesture for himself. A moment later,
he again reveals his sensitivity to any nuance of expression in

Rogozhin's features when he observes, "Here you are looking at me with hatred!" (201), an observation that is later repeated in almost the same words ("How dreadfully you look at me now!" 208), expressing the same horror. Later, the reader is again made cognizant of Myshkin's immediate response to Rogozhin's gestural "language," when the prince's thoughts ("don't frown. And why do you laugh?" 354) are parenthetically conveyed, in answer to Rogozhin's constantly shifting moods, haplessly reflected on a visage that can only mirror the passion and gloom that lies within.

At one point, Myshkin and Rogozhin meet briefly late at night in the park at Pavlovsk. The prince is startled by his "rival's" sudden, unexpected appearance.

> Myshkin could not for some time collect his thoughts, and an agonizing sensation rose up again in his heart. Rogozhin saw the effect he had produced, but although he was at first taken aback and talked with an air of studied ease, Myshkin fancied soon that there was nothing studied about him, nor even any special embarrassment. If there were any awkwardness in his gestures and words, it was only on the surface. The man could not change at heart. (352)

Once more each takes the measure of the other ("Rogozhin saw the effect he had produced"). Again, we are told how Myshkin interprets both Rogozhin's speech and gesture, as related but distinct semiotic orders, meriting critical attention that accords with the considered analysis articulated in the novel.

At a moment when the prince implores Rogozhin to remember that they have exchanged crosses in symbolic recognition of their intended bond, Myshkin asks: "Why do you turn away from me? Why do you hide your hand?" Shortly thereafter, the reader is told that, in fact, "He had moved two steps away, and was actually standing with his face averted from Myshkin and his hands hidden behind him" (353). Here Myshkin's troubled

queries, rendered as metaphoric speech, are readily transformed into expressive gestural activity, as the interplay of speech
and gesture becomes realized metaphor, and Myshkin's figurative expression is manifested in Rogozhin's chilling response.

When asked about the possibility of there being a love
interest in his life, the prince awkwardly responds: "'What,
what could you have heard?' Myshkin started, and stopped in
extreme confusion." Rogozhin, in turn, quickly interprets the
significance not of the words he hears but of the gestures he
sees: "And I've not merely heard it; I see now it's true" (354).
His immediate understanding confirms once again that not
only is the world of fiction replete with signs that are both
verbal and nonverbal, as in the actual world, but that the latter
mode of (unwitting) communication may occasionally achieve
primacy as the principal means for getting at the truth.

In each of these instances, gesture, as a sign requiring
interpretation, is clearly an inherent semiotic feature of the
given dialogue. The same is true, moreover, of those highly
charged moments of silence—semantically weighted as meaning-
bearing events—that interlace their speech, stockpiling tension
rather than dissipating it.

> They were silent for a while. (200)

> Both were silent again. (201)

> Rogozhin bent a lowering, terrible gaze on Myshkin
> and made no answer. . . . he went on after a minute.
> (203)

> They were silent for five minutes. (590)

> They were silent for a long time. (593)

Each time, the moment of silence is almost palpable, and is
conveyed to the reader as such. The stillness is that produced

by a consciousness in the process of formulating speech—and thereby attempting to deal with the world and its challenges.

During the several meetings between Myshkin and Rogozhin, the dialogue always concentrates on the one single subject: her. Nastasya Filippovna is never named by either of them. There is no need to ascertain the subject for it is fixed by Rogozhin's obsession. In effect, their talk gravitates around his single-minded passion which gives their dialogue its sole reason for being. Once she is dead, there is no longer any need for talk, and, indeed, it gradually dissipates. Their final meeting occurs in Rogozhin's gloomy quarters where the powerful intimation of dark forces at work is finally realized. The demonic secret, which the house has harbored all along, finally and paradoxically becomes incarnate in Nastasya Filippovna's corpse. Wrapped in a white sheet, her motionless body inspires the all night vigil in which dialogue steadily deteriorates into an all-pervading, conclusive silence.

A terrible destiny foreshadowed at their first meeting comes full circle at their last; premonition, following its own peculiar laws, comes to sad fruition. Insight combined with foresight—that perceptive ability displayed by an especially gifted (frequently abnormal) figure—serves to anticipate the death of Nastasya Filippovna, as Myshkin repeatedly gives voice to, and yet at the same time rejects, the premonition of danger for the woman they both love.

> "Well, there's no distinguishing your love from hate,"
> said Myshkin, smiling. "It will pass, and then perhaps
> the trouble will be worse. I tell you this . . . "
> "That I shall murder her?" (206)

In response, the prince shudders; he cannot bring himself to credit what he himself has already uttered once and will now say again. "Any man would be better than you, because you really may murder her . . . " Rogozhin not only carefully listens to every word but observes, in turn, every fleeting nuance of expression. "Rogozhin . . . was watching every movement, every change in Myshkin's face with extraordinary intentness" (206). Shortly thereafter, the prince returns to the theme which obsesses him: "Of course she doesn't think so ill of you as you say. If she did, it would be as good as deliberately going to be drowned or murdered to marry you" (208). When only a few moments later Myshkin picks up Rogozhin's knife, completing gesturally the premonition he has previously expressed verbally, he examines it with inordinate curiosity. Rogozhin twice takes it out of his hands, as Myshkin's unconscious but increasing preoccupation with the object evokes the other's wrath. "'Can't I buy a new knife?' Rogozhin cried in a perfect frenzy, growing more exasperated at every word." The prince trembles as he stares fixedly at his host with no other response forthcoming. "Myshkin started and looked intently at Rogozhin" (210). The dual gestures enacted in silence signify that the prince cannot bear to acknowledge what he understands all too well. On essentially that note (and with that despairing gesture), the discussion ends. But Myshkin himself will come very close to feeling the cutting edge of that knife, while Nastasya Filippovna is destined to fall under its sharp blade—an eventuality which is foreshadowed by the expressive language of gesture that is as communicative in Dostoevskian dialogue as its complementary verbal mode.

Once fate has taken its course, Rogozhin seeks out Myshkin so that they—and the woman—may finally be together. Rogozhin's voice significantly never rises above a whisper, as though he were now, and for all time, in the presence of the dead. He is fully absorbed in the mystery which he intends to reveal to the "brother" with whom he has exchanged crosses. Myshkin, too, is subdued, and only hesitantly poses the same fearful question at crucial moments, each time afraid to learn what he already knows. Thus, on the way to Rogozhin's, he still manages to keep that terrible knowledge at a safe distance, as he asks:

> "Is Nastasya Filippovna in your house?"
> "Yes." (587)

Once in Rogozhin's quarters, however, the fear of having his own premonition realized begins to take hold.

> "Where is . . . Nastasya Filippovna?" Myshkin articu-
> lated breathlessly.
> "She is . . . here," Rogozhin brought out slowly, after
> a moment's delay. (588)

Finally, Myshkin is desperate to confront the truth which he prays is a lie.

> "Rogozhin! Where is Nastasya Filippovna?" Myshkin
> whispered suddenly, and he stood up trembling in
> every limb.
> "There," he whispered, nodding towards the curtain.
> (589)

Each step towards Rogozhin's house and within has taken Myshkin closer to what had been inevitable and is now irrevocable. Thus, the truth appears gradually, as it effects a kind of centripetal force on the novel's protagonist, drawing him with fateful insistence toward an existential abyss and madness. Myshkin is never told she is dead, nor is the reader; the prince eventually sees for himself, the latter learns by virtue of a telling silence.

> Neither of them uttered a word all the while they stood
> by the bedside . . . in the death-like silence of the
> room. . . . Myshkin looked and felt that as he looked,

> the room became more and more still and death-like.
> (589-90)

A kind of fearful metonym, the deathly silence alone signifies that there is death in the room.

Their last meeting is conducted in whispered tones. Both men are awed by the woman's silent presence. Rogozhin becomes increasingly lost in thought. Meanwhile, the prince had begun to tremble and seems never to stop.

> ... all at once, for some reason, Myshkin began trembling. (587)

> Myshkin shuddered. (590)

> Myshkin trembled more and more violently. .. (590)

His agitation becomes so acute, Rogozhin is moved (in several instances) to remark upon it. "'I wonder about you, you keep trembling . . . . What's the matter, can't you stand up?' Rogozhin asked with apprehensive wonder, seeing that Myshkin was trembling so much that he could not get up" (591). In response to Myshkin's few questions, he provides distractedly the details of her murder. Finally, his speech becomes entirely disoriented, while there is nothing left for Myshkin to ask, nor for Rogozhin to explain. The prince can only rise and be seated again, and render a gesture expressive of the awe he feels, the horror, and the end. "He stood up and wrung his hands" (593). As each recedes into his own private despair, words yield to hopeless gestures until all that is left of their dialogue is dead silence. The prince can only stroke the cheeks of his friend who is slipping into temporary insanity, while he himself slips even further away.

*

In *Crime and Punishment*, a series of alternating dialogues yield several climactic scenes. Raskolnikov meets three times with the detective Porfiry and, alternately, has three talks with the young prostitute Sonya. Throughout the novel he is continually going from one to the other. Meeting first with the detective, he sees the girl last before taking up his cross. During his second visit to Sonya, he reveals that he is the murderer of her friend Lizaveta; while at the crucial moment in his final meeting with Porfiry, the latter informs Raskolnikov that he knows the student has killed the old pawnbroker and her sister. Raskolnikov thus receives that very same information from the detective that he had earlier imparted to the girl, making his role pivotal within the circular traffic of information that communicates to both protagonist and reader that there is no rationale for murder and no escape from the mark of Cain. Raskolnikov tells neither Porfiry nor Sonya directly that he is responsible for the crime, yet both arrive at the same correct conclusion. Although each is able to judge partly on the basis of Raskolnikov's revealing utterances, their individual realizations of the fact are also determined by the "expressive gesture" which plays a crucial role in both series of talks.

At the first meeting between student and detective, Raskolnikov enters Porfiry's quarters engulfed in spasms of uncontrollable laughter. He does so to communicate at once that a person in such evident high spirits is surely at peace with himself and the world. Ironically, his ploy does not achieve its intended effect, but serves the detective instead, who sees through the obvious gesture to the possibility of hidden intent, as Raskolnikov will learn at the end. "Your laughter, that laughter of yours as you came in . . . why, I guessed everything then, I saw it all quite plainly . . . " (434). Thus Raskolnikov's initial gesture, falsely played, betrays the inexperienced youth and provides the detective his first clue.

Others follow—on both the verbal and gestural planes. First, the wily Porfiry extracts from his guest the details of a theory that tolerates murder when enacted by select individuals in extenuating circumstances. Can this draggletailed student possibly consider himself such an individual, wonders the astute detective. In seeking an answer, he masterfully engages his young interlocutor on a parallel plane of nonverbal communication, whose import is refracted through the sympathetic consciousness of Razumikhin, who witnesses more than he is able to understand.

> Raskolnikov did not answer, but silently lifted towards him his pale and almost sorrowful face. And it seemed to Razumikhin that Porfiry's ill-concealed, obtrusive, irritating, and unmannerly causticity contrasted strangely with that calm and melancholy face. (253)

What the unwitting Razumikhin observes here and earlier ("Even before this he had begun to notice something." 255) are the hidden nuances of meaning concealed in those sidelong glances, mocking expressions, and bits of outright laughter that permeate the confrontation between student and detective. That these are signs to be interpreted is underscored, in this instance, by the novelist's insistent usage—highlighted further by the italics at the end—of a distinctly unwieldy string of adjectives (that are even more noticeably burdensome in the original Russian: *neskryvaemaja, navjazčivaja, razdražitel'- naja i nevežlivaja*). In effect, the reader is asked to take cognizance of this second mode of communication which may at times, by virtue of its own semantic weight, take precedence over the otherwise more tangible verbal interaction.

In gauging his opponent, within the drama of this subtle hidden duel, Raskolnikov strains ("trying hard to make his voice tremble") for a poignant effect, when he mentions his father's watch which he had been obliged to pawn. Afterward, he wonders if he has achieved a sympathetic effect. "Have I done well? Did it seem natural? Wasn't it too exaggerated?" (241). A moment later, however, he shudders—unintentionally— upon learning that Porfiry has in fact been expecting him. Engaged in the same muted effort to impart and receive gestural information, the detective purposely chooses not to notice or comment upon Raskolnikov's obvious reaction. "Raskolnikov started, but Porfiry . . . appeared not to see him" (242). On other occasions, however, when eschewing delicacy is very much a part of his strategy, Porfiry is careful to remark upon the former student's obvious discomfiture both gesturally ("Raskolnikov's whole body quivered, so that Porfiry Petrovich took obvious note of it" 334) and verbally ("Look, I declare he's trembling" 443). The two are thus engaged in the same game, with the stakes clear to both, if different for each.

At the start of their second meeting, Raskolnikov is immediately obliged to interpret his opponent's gestures. "He held out both his hands to me, but he didn't actually give me one; he drew them back in time." At the same time, the reader is informed of the struggle's silent progress. "They were each watching the other, but as soon as their glances met, both turned their eyes away like lightning" (319). This kind of engagement and immediate withdrawal also has its special significance. At certain moments, Porfiry purposely keeps his eyes turned away ("as before, apparently trying to avoid meeting his guest's eyes" 322), while at others, even a "casual" glance from him causes the student to be on the alert. "'But you were really quite right,' Porfiry began again gaily, looking at Raskolnikov with extraordinary artlessness (which made him start and instantly prepare himself for something)" (324). In their talk, a look is made to bear import and elicit a reaction, even parenthetically.

During this second interview, Porfiry seems never to remain still. Constantly in motion, he is likened to a little round ball careening off the corners and walls of his office. Finally, his disconcerting mobility ("He was almost running about the room" 324) inspires an apology and curious explanation ("haemorrhoids, you know" 323), which do not discredit the likely possibility that this is just another tactic designed to unnerve his highly volatile interlocutor. For by using to advantage his ungainly figure and absurd appearance, along with his remarkable ability to gush verbal torrents at will, the detective's aim is to cause his quarry to flare up and reveal himself. For his part, Raskolnikov realizes that his best strategy is silence.

> At moments he longed to throw himself on Porfiry and strangle him then and there. From the time he entered he had been afraid of his own rage. He was conscious of his dry lips flecked with foam, and of his hammering heart. But he was determined not to say a word until the right time came. He knew this to be the best tactic in his position. (327)

As a communicative gesture, laughter is utilized by both duelists—but generally works to the advantage of Porfiry, who chuckles seemingly without pause. When he explains in detail his theory that a criminal intellect of a certain stamp is always sure to give itself away, Raskolnikov, who recognizes himself in Porfiry's hypothetical construct, appears like a frightened creature at bay. Although thoroughly mirthless, he attempts to dissimulate by utilizing laughter to his own purposes. But his awkward, convulsive attempt is immediately interrupted and cut short by a similar burst of feigned amusement on the part of the detective. Having acquired the advantage, Porfiry manages to give the disturbing impression that he is laughing at his guest, a tactic which succeeds in throwing the latter entirely off balance.

> "If you find that you have a legal right to prosecute me or arrest me, then do it! But I will not permit anyone to laugh in my face and torment me . . . "

> His lips began to tremble, his eyes shone with fury, and
> his voice rose, although he had been trying to keep it
> low. "I will not permit it," he shouted, banging his fist
> violently on the table. "Do you hear that, Porfiry
> Petrovich? I will not permit it!" (329)

The detective's efforts are consistently launched against the
other's Achilles' heel—his pride. As a means of probing and
irritating a sensitive area, what finally breaks the student's
resolve to remain silent and aloof is Porfiry's mocking laughter,
which proves sufficient as a crude but effective instrument.

Porfiry's most characteristic gesture, however, is his per-
sistent, seemingly knowing wink. The first time the detective
screws up his eye, apparently winking at him, Raskolnikov
immediately interprets the gesture as indicative of Porfiry's
intuitive understanding of more than he lets on: "'He knows!'
flashed through his brain like lightning" (241). Another clever,
disconcerting device, this also works in the detective's favor—
until the very moment of reckoning, when he proclaims Raskolnikov the murderer. In the painful interim, as his principal
strategy, Porfiry causes speech and gesture to clash by playing
one against the other ("making gestures that were always extraordinarily out of keeping with his words" 324), with the aim
of having one communicative mode consistently contradict or
cancel out the other. In this manner, Porfiry actively effects
the disorienting ambiguity which characterizes his end of the
dialogue, and which leaves the student in constant turmoil and
uncertainty.

> "'A wondrous thing, wondrous . . . ' repeated Porfiry
> Petrovich, as if he had begun to think of something
> else. 'Yes, wondrous!' he almost shouted at last, sud-
> denly turning his eyes on Raskolnikov and coming to
> a stop two paces away from him. There was something
> stupid and trivial about this constant repetition that

> contrasted strongly with the serious, contemplative,
> and enigmatic look he now bent on his visitor.
> All this still further intensified Raskolnikov's bitter
> malice, and he could no longer resist issuing an ironical
> and rather indiscreet challenge. (320-21)

> "He seemed to be growing ever more high-spirited and
> playful, and this made Raskolnikov finally lose
> control" (335).

Porfiry's vexatious playfulness, his employment of banal speech coupled with penetrating glances, his affinity for making statements which are immediately contradicted by an accompanying look and, finally, his taking a seemingly frivolous attitude toward a matter of the utmost seriousness all contribute to infuriate Raskolnikov, whose consistent response, then, is to compromise repeatedly his own position.

Thus the detective challenges the proud intellectual with a varied arsenal of disconcerting moves, which in turn evoke anger and careless revelations. These tend to confirm the detective's initial supposition. For Porfiry has turned the contrastive and contradictory interplay of speech and gesture into a fine art, which he utilizes professionally to achieve his ends; in this case, to elicit a confession from a hapless student, seduced by an idea which he carries out to an inauspicious conclusion.

Porfiry's inane verbosity is always in conflict with the seriousness—even in laughter—of his constantly probing gestural activity. In contrast, during the meetings between the student and prostitute, the expressiveness of Sonya's features reinforces her utterances:

> "What should I do without God?" she said in a rapid,
> forceful whisper, glancing at him for a moment out of

suddenly flashing eyes, and pressing his hand with hers. (311)

Or, they communicate what she cannot express verbally:

> Her pale cheeks had flushed again, and her eyes looked full of anguish. She was plainly very deeply moved, and longing to speak, to plead, to find expression for something. An almost *insatiable* compassion . . . was depicted in every feature of her face. (305)

Sonya is essentially incapable of articulating what she feels most deeply. Hence the dialogue between the two routinely incorporates (as illustrated by the two instances just cited, respectively) gesture as a supportive mode of communication in conjunction with speech, or nonverbal modes depicted as her sole means of communication at a given moment. Yet her inability to speak, partly compensated for by her special insight, is complemented by Raskolnikov's own perspicuity. Reflecting the girl's innermost thoughts and feelings, her gestures in virtually all instances are comprehended and interpreted by the student.

> He had read it all in her look. (309)

> . . . and this was evident to him. (309)

> And it was only now that he fully comprehended . . . (309)

> . . . it was clear, again . . . (310)

> . . . he could see that; it was her real self that stood before him . . . (310)

> He could see all this in her eyes and in her emotional agitation . . . (313)

The entire process—her gesturing, his understanding—is thus refracted through Raskolnikov's consciousness and interpolated for the reader. Finally, in a moment of stark recognition, he perceives that her entire visage, the totality of her look, is expressive of a single, overwhelming and incontestable fact: "'Yurodivaya! yurodivaya!'[8] he repeated firmly to himself" (311).

While Porfiry's characteristic gestures are a perpetual wink and a seemingly irrepressible chuckle, both employed as intentional devices, Sonya is continually (upwards of ten times in as many pages) wringing her hands in despair—over the plight of others: Katerina Ivanovna, the children, Raskolnikov. By arguing against God's good intentions toward these others, the rationalistic student reduces the inarticulate girl to helpless gestures.

> She had listened with an imploring face, with her eyes on him and her hands clasped in silent supplication, as though it all depended on him. (308)

His subsequent observation that perhaps God does not even exist leaves her tortured and speechless.

> Sonya's face underwent a sudden and awful change; a tremor passed over it. She looked at him with inexpressible reproach; she tried to say something, but she could not utter a word, and only covered her face with her hands and sobbed bitterly. (308)

But Raskolnikov himself is suffering an even worse despair which is also manifested in a gesture, as he kneels to kiss her foot. In response to her visible horror at his action, he explains—affording gesture its explicit verbal interpretation—that his act is performed in recognition of the suffering of all humanity. "I prostrated myself not before you, but before all human suffering" (309).

At the end of their first talk, Raskolnikov promises to tell Sonya at their next meeting who has committed the murder. When he appears on the following day, he transmits the information to her by an intently fixed glance that demands that she perceive and comprehend—without his verbalizing it—what she does not want to understand.

> He turned to her and steadily, steadily, looked at her.
> A convulsive shudder shook her.
> . . . Raskolnikov [continued] to keep his eyes fixed on her face, as though it were not in his power to turn them away.
> Another terrible minute went by. They still gazed at one another. (393)

As a consequence of that "terrible" extended period of silence, Sonya finally understands that he is the murderer by "reading" the fact on his suffering features ("she stared at him for some time and then . . . . 'Oh God!' burst in a terrible wail from her breast" 393-94). From the despair on his face, she understands with the kind of perspecuity characteristic of the *yurodivaya* not only what he has perpetrated but also the extent of the damage. "What have you done, what have you done to yourself?" (394). Recoiling in horror at the wordless revelation, her first reaction is to distance herself from him, yet she almost immediately returns to his side, and in a frenzy throws herself on her knees before him—echoing and responding to his earlier gesture. Then taking his hands in hers, she expresses both by this gesture and in words her determination never to part from him. Not only in this instance, however, but during all their talks, and perhaps more so than elsewhere in the novels, words alone seem never to suffice. The language of expressive gesture is instead repeatedly and consistently employed by the girl, and then interpreted by the student—who, in turn, demands that she interpret the terrible truth without his uttering a single word.

Crime, within the novelist's vision, is perpetrated against oneself as well as against another. With the peculiar insight endowed her, Sonya perceives this immediately as an unmitigated truth. Raskolnikov, the intellectual, learns it only gradually, but already knows it full well when he proclaims to Sonya at their second meeting: "I killed myself, not that old woman!" (402). In essence, this learning process, culminating in the realization that to violate a member of the human community is to violate oneself, is what the novel is all about.

*

In this chapter, we have argued that, as components of Dostoevskian dialogue, modes of nonverbal communication in general, embracing silence and gesture in particular, transform that dialogue into drama, making it synonymous with and a part of the action itself. To demonstrate this with regard to Dostoevsky's last novel, the three interviews between Ivan and Smerdyakov will be surveyed briefly from this single standpoint. Here, too, as tension mounts, culminating in Smerdyakov's startling revelation, the changing relations between the two interlocutors may again be charted by paying close attention to the language of gesture.

At the first meeting between master and servant, a sickly Smerdyakov curiously retains his former aspect only through an uncontrollable twitch in one eye. The disfiguring feature instantly triggers for Ivan the recollection of the lackey's discomforting formula which, as he eventually learns, represents in the mind of Smerdyakov a virtual license to murder.

> But in the left eye, which was screwed up and seemed
> to be insinuating something, Smerdyakov showed him-
> self unchanged. "It's always worthwhile speaking to a
> clever man." Ivan was reminded of that at once. (573)

That key phrase, an ironic complement to Ivan's own formulaic expression ("Everything is permitted") promoting the extreme exercise of free will, figures as an important point of contention in the dialogue to follow. At this stage, Smerdyakov's leering euphemism for concealed but shared ill will is resurrected only by a raised and twitching eyebrow—a gesture that communicates more information than Ivan wants to receive.

For Smerdyakov, Ivan's visit is superfluous; to his criminal intellect everything had already been decided. During the course of their first brief meeting, his continued displeasure is conveyed repeatedly by a reluctance to speak. Upon receiving his guest, therefore, the lackey persistently maintains his silence, designed to express his dissatisfaction and unwillingness to delve into—what he deems—closed matters.

> Smerdyakov . . . was not the first to speak. He remained dumb, and did not even look much interested. (573)

> Smerdyakov sighed. (573)

> Smerdyakov was stolidly silent for a while. (573)

> Smerdyakov . . . was again silent for a minute. (575)

> Smerdyakov sighed again and again. (576)

> He slowly ceased speaking . . . (577)

Although all these signs would suggest otherwise, Ivan allows his mind to be set at rest ("you have calmed me" 577), and departs.

At their second meeting, however, Ivan is immediately infuriated at the sight of his former lackey in spectacles—and, even more so, by the insolent gesture employed to remove them.

> "A creature like that and wearing spectacles!" Smer-
> dyakov slowly raised his head and looked intently at
> his visitor through his spectacles; then he slowly took
> them off and rose from the bench, but by no means
> respectfully, almost lazily, doing the least possible re-
> quired by common civility. All this struck Ivan instant-
> ly, he took it all in and noted it all at once—most of all
> the look in Smerdyakov's eyes, positively malicious,
> churlish, and haughty. "What do you want to intrude
> for?" it seemed to say; "we settled everything then,
> why have you come again?" Ivan could scarcely control
> himself. (580-81)

The meaning of the gesture is thus filtered through Ivan's
consciousness and interpreted for the reader. At the same time,
that gesture, together with the reaction it inspires, sets the
tone for the entire ensuing dialogue, in which Ivan's fury is
represented at first by hands which tremble and then by
clenched fists pounding on the table top. Eventually,
Smerdyakov's haughty retreats into silence and recurrent insolent stare, expressing resentment at his former master's
probing, result in that same fist being raised against him, as
gesture for the moment is transformed into violence. But in
this—their second—meeting, transformations occur rapidly,
and it is not long before the tables are turned, as Ivan, becoming
gradually incapacitated by the force of the contentions raised
against him, is reduced to an object of his lackey's scorn—all of
which is captured in the now reversed postures of master and
man. Previously self-assertive, the former becomes passive (and
his hands, inactive), while the latter begins to enjoy a new
status in their confrontation.

>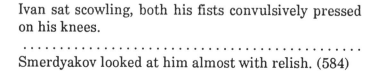
> Ivan sat scowling, both his fists convulsively pressed
> on his knees.
> . . . .
> Smerdyakov looked at him almost with relish. (584)

To complete the reversal, by the end of their meeting, it is Ivan who finds himself invoking the lackey's own expression as a means to understanding, only now having been struck by its remarkable adaptability and ambiguity: "'That's as much as to say "It's always worthwhile speaking to a clever man,"eh?' snarled Ivan" (584). Having thus recognized the power and persuasiveness of the other's argument, Ivan gathers up his belongings and leaves as he entered—trembling, but for the moment, with no further word.

During their third and final meeting, Ivan finds his former lackey even less responsive than before, as their dialogue is once again initiated by Smerdyakov's obstinate silence.

> He met Ivan with a slow silent gaze . . .
> Smerdyakov still remained silent, looking quietly at
> Ivan as before. Suddenly, he waved his hand and
> turned his face away. (589)

Nevertheless, he is finally obliged to respond to the other's fearful questioning. Smerdyakov's revelation that Ivan had authored—and he, as instrument, had carried out—the father's murder represents the stunning climax to their dialogue. Yet the tense interaction between interlocutors, culminating in Ivan's dazed and startled reception of the information, may be documented without reference to a single word uttered by either.

> . . . turning his face to Ivan again, [Smerdyakov] stared
> at him with a look of frenzied hatred, the same look
> that he had fixed on him at their last interview, a
> month before.
> . . . .
> [Smerdyakov] smiled contemptuously and suddenly
> laughed outright.
> . . . .
> Smerdyakov stared at him almost with revulsion. (589)
> . . . .

Smerdyakov measured him with his eyes.

. . . .

Ivan looked at him speechless.

. . . .

Ivan shuddered.

. . . .

Ivan jumped up and seized him by the shoulder.

. . . .

Smerdyakov was not in the least scared. He only riveted his eyes on Ivan with insane hatred.

. . . .

Ivan sank back on his chair, as though pondering something. He laughed malignantly.

. . . .

Something seemed to give way in his brain, and he shuddered all over with a cold shiver. Then Smerdyakov himself looked at him wonderingly; probably the genuineness of Ivan's horror struck him. (590)

By thus simply isolating and recording the so-called "dumb show," it becomes strikingly evident just how expressive it is.

In sum, our intent has been to show the density and proliferation of devices grounded in modes of nonverbal communication as prominent features of Dostoevskian dialogue. Typically in narrative art, a character's aspect reveals a gesture frozen in novelistic time that requires interpretation as part—or in lieu—of a given speech act. Gestural activity that is described as immediately accompanying an utterance, or that is seen to be manifested exclusively in the absence of speech, will clearly bear meaning. Significantly, in dialogue authored by Dostoevsky, the import of what remains unuttered or only gestured is of the same potential importance as the speech itself, or may even exceed the semantic weight of what is actually said.

From a hitherto neglected perspective, this view affords additional affirmation of the wealth of explicit detail comprising Dostoevskian dialogue. Further, it recognizes that, as a distinctive feature of this dialogue, crucial information is often conveyed *solely* nonverbally—by an intense look or nuance of expression, by feigned (or real) laughter, a winking left eye, an uncontrolled trembling extremity, or by some other physical detail. As signs acknowledged and interpreted by the characters engaged in dialogue, they receive immediate verbal or gestural response. Dostoevsky's interlocutors thus strain to read one another's features and to understand the veiled or ill-concealed gestures that are accompanied by an utterance or thought-filled silence. Their efforts at interpretation demand a similar act on the part of the reader, who is called upon to recognize that in such dialogue there is a secondary, essentially gestural mode of communication that is interwoven within, and supportive of, the verbal interaction that is generally primary.

3

The Poetics of Absence

The Idiot; The Possessed

The preceding chapter discusses structures of silence. While the absence of speech is implicitly acknowledged as being requisite to their formation, such structures, in the present context, are not understood solely in terms of absence. Rather, silence represents a value of its own, a mode of (nonverbal) communication that is both dynamic and specific—but not unique—to the Dostoevsky novel. Silence, in other words, bears a certain inherent potential semantic weight. In Dostoevsky, that potential is realized as something almost palpable within the dialogic relations of his characters. Similarly, thematic and ideological substance may be borne not only by the absence of dialogue but, more inclusively, by the absence of drama. Yet this sense of "absence" entails as well a positive value determined by strategic omission. As realized in *The Idiot* and *The Possessed*, respectively, that type of strategy comprises the present topic.

If the novel as genre is acknowledged to represent structures that afford fictional communication among characters, then *The Idiot* is remarkable for its pronounced lack of communication among its principal characters. More specifically, this novel's fundamental tensions frequently and conclusively derive from the characters' *non*-communication. In accordance with narrative technique in general, much is left hidden or obscured in the novel, whose fictional world is conventionally governed by the tensions generated between the mimetic and diegetic—between what is dramatized as detailed event and what is told the reader as reported incident.

Comprised of interwoven mimetic and diegetic modes of representation set in complementary opposition, the narrative text commonly exhibits both to varying degree alternately. Representing direct character interaction, the former mode necessarily incorporates direct speech within passages that are both active and dramatic. By contrast, as authorial report, the diegetic mode is determined by functions that are at once descriptive and informative. Affording summary and commentary, it is characterized by a virtually complete absence of dramatized events, only minimal interaction among characters, resulting in the near absence of dialogue. Composed largely of authorial accounts, periodically enhanced by a character's utterances, embedded as isolated fragments of reported speech, affording added detail, there is in such instances a high reduction of drama in favor of a more economical report to the reader. Paradoxically, in a novel as "dramatic" as *The Idiot*, this mode of narrative representation is crucial to its strategies of suspense and climactic event.

In the entire novel there is only a single brief scene where Prince Myshkin and Nastasya Filippovna, the principal male and female protagonists, are depicted alone together. She accosts him after midnight in the park at Pavlovsk, falls on her knees before him, and tries unsuccessfully to kiss his hands. He raises her from the ground in horror. After a moment's frenzied talk, an embittered Rogozhin appears from the shadows and escorts her from the site. The only other occasions where Myshkin is given to converse with Nastasya Filippovna at all are at her name day party in the opening scenes and during the single meeting between the two women of the novel at the end. Rogozhin's appearance in the park parallels, moreover, an earlier one in which he ushers Nastasya Filippovna away from the scene after she strikes a young officer in the face with a riding whip. These two fleeting moments are likewise the only instances in the entire work when Nastasya Filippovna and her fateful suitor are shown alone together. On neither occasion, however, do they utter a single word to one another. In sum, these few dramatized scenes represent the novel's distinctly isolated instances in which its three major characters engage in what amounts to exceptionally minimal interaction. This delimiting aspect of the work becomes all the more remarkable upon consideration of the fact that the whole action of the novel revolves around the highly volatile triangle composed of an idiot prince, an obsessive bourgeois, and a death-seeking, impassioned female desperately straining to distance herself from her past, while deliberately challenging all and sundry by proclaiming a liberated present.[1]

The novel centers on the figure of Myshkin, who is planted squarely in the midst of chaotic events over which he has no control. Almost immediately upon his arrival in Petersburg he is placed at the vortex of coincidentally related incidents churned by greed, suspicion, and lust. In this pivotal role, Myshkin actualizes the novel's governing idea, embodied in the well-intentioned yet hardly benign prince, whose presence and contradictory behavior fires Rogozhin's perverse imagination to distraction and murder. In awesome paradox, the vicious circle of the novel is defined and sustained by Myshkin's fear of what will become of Nastasya Filippovna, keeping him close on her trail, and thus substantially contributing to her terrible end. Yet to suggest that Myshkin with all his insight has not the wisdom to remove himself from the scene would be tantamount to observing that Ahab might just as well have left the white whale alone, since the novel's fundamental conception demands that the prince be at the center struggling to maintain his own equilibrium among forces and personalities beyond his ken. As a further paradox, however, being in the vortex leaves him estranged and distanced from Nastasya Filippovna, with whom he is almost exclusively occupied. The same observation, moreover, might be legitimately applied to Rogozhin as well, for the reader is provided no more than a fleeting glance at either man alone with the woman—until the triangle is finally completed in the linked mysteries of madness and death.

Myshkin and Rogozhin, by contrast, meet on several occasions, notably at the latter's house (twice) and in the park at Pavlovsk (twice), to talk about the woman who unites them as brothers of the cross and suffering, as one very nearly the victim of the other, and as sacrifices at a shrine to Beauty distorted and damned. But within the structural framework of the novel, each "suitor" must content himself with learning about Nastasya Filippovna from the other—a principal device of the novel which, in effect, allows the reader to learn from both, but to see little at firsthand. Myshkin thus recounts for Rogozhin what takes place—and, just as important, what does not—between him and the other's betrothed, providing Rogozhin and the reader with her most striking utterances. In reciprocal fashion, Rogozhin offers like information centering on the terrible trials of his great, all-consuming, but uncompassionate love. Meanwhile, as the focus of the extended discussion, the devastated beauty herself rarely appears—and then more like a phantom or apparition than as flesh and blood; more often, it seems, in Myshkin's dreams than in his reality. Indeed, the conception of her as phantom-like is further suggested by the fact that so little blood is let from her fatal wound. She appears, then, almost bloodless, seeking her lost purity, passionate only in her grief at having been wronged, and yet truly compelling in her headlong rush to destruction. Paralleling Myshkin's central place in the action of the novel (he is present in virtually every scene), Nastasya Filippovna occupies a focal position in the dialogue of its characters. Desired by some, disdained by others, hurt but unchastened, she attains by virtue of her sustained absence and special aura an importance rivaling Myshkin's presence. Ultimately, their roles are complementary; she is present in the minds and thoughts of others to the same degree that he is suddenly thrust into their lives. Everyone in the novel is preoccupied with one, the other, or both.

The meeting between Aglaya and Myshkin at the green bench in Pavlovsk illustrates the point. Echoing the earlier scene in the novel at Rogozhin's, this time the prince and the other young beauty talk only about *her*. In ironic reversal of the theme, Aglaya now renders Myshkin an account of his own adventures with Nastasya Filippovna (as he had previously done for Rogozhin), while he in turn further expands, objects, and exhorts. As a result of this proliferated mode of report, crucial episodes are purposefully left undramatized and are only partially *told*, thereby attaining their own level of importance in a narrative which, by omitting as much as it explains, achieves a profound sense of mystery in the process. What is couched in drama as an event taking place within the temporal bounds of the plot proper is thus implicitly juxtaposed to what is described or related as having occurred "earlier and elsewhere." The obvious implication and intent is that what remains "unseen" by the reader is left to much greater degree unknown than what has been depicted by the novelist or "shown."

In the one case, the characters' "present" interaction is conceived as being contemporaneous with its exposition.[2] The other represents a report of what had transpired at some other time and place. One mode may be equated with an essentially bare descriptive account devoid of dialogic interaction; the other depicts the characters' dramatic engagement.[3] Myshkin's arrival by train to St. Petersburg in cloak and gaiters with two newly made acquaintances represents an instance of the latter. The reader is presented it all in dramatic detail as the novel opens. Told to an ostensible audience, by contrast, Myshkin's expansive account of his experiences in Switzerland are not a part of the novel's present concerns. Conforming with this common narrative model, *The Idiot* is composed of two interlarded layers of discourse. Presented in fully developed dramatic detail, the series of events depicted at the moment of their occurrence comprise the novel's plot proper or fictive present. Of present concern, however, are those episodes that are left undramatized as a fundamental constraint. Temporally and spatially displaced, they remain by careful design beyond the reader's purview—until the moment for their critically delayed *telling*.

As information which comes to light at the appropriate moment, allowing the plot to progress from one stage to the next, those passages which detail what happens outside the novel's temporal and spatial bounds serve to motivate a later sequence of events. The causal-sequential chain of events underlying the plot of the novel, in other words, is repeatedly initiated by events occurring outside the series of dramatized episodes comprising the surface plot presented the reader. Major events orchestrated beyond or occurring entirely outside that series include Nastasya Filippovna's early years in the country, Myshkin's life in Switzerland, the manner by which he comes into an inheritance in Russia, Rogozhin's adventures with Nastasya Filippovna, paralleled by Myshkin's, and concluding with her death. All of these require separate detailed accounts. Each is the source of profound ramifications either within the characters' volatile set of relationships, ever on the brink of dissolution, or within the individual character's equally fragile psychological composition.

Similarly, a whole series of less important episodes also take place off-stage or have their causes rooted there. Thus, General Ivolgin's theft of the four-hundred rubles (which ultimately leads to his demise), Nastasya Filippovna's charges of shady financial dealings (which evoke a series of responsive explanations from Yevgeny Pavlovich to Myshkin), Burdovsky's false claim to a portion of Myshkin's inheritance (to be further discussed below), and, more important, the letters sent by

Nastasya Filippovna to Aglaya (which serve as the ostensible cause for their meeting) all represent such instances. What these episodes share in common is the need, initially, for their greater elaboration. Yet, whether of major or minor consequence, these partially revealing accounts serve as the individual sources from which the subsequent action of the novel emanates. Through descriptive report, they provide both the motivation and rationale for their dramatic counterpart.

What the reader is not shown, in other words, counts for as much in the total aesthetic and dramatic effect as what is made part of his purview. He is intrigued by the thought of Nastasya Filippovna's running from Myshkin, who wants to save her, to Rogozhin, who can only destroy her, as all three know, and back to Myshkin again. Myshkin learns that Nastasya Filippovna repeatedly deserts Rogozhin "right from under the wedding canopy"; that Rogozhin has beaten her and has humbly, pathetically begged forgiveness; and that he suffers what he can only regard as further humiliation at her hands, which he fully intends to repay. Rogozhin learns that Myshkin and Nastasya Filippovna remain separate when together and that Myshkin loves her "not with love but with compassion." The reader thus acquires information from both. And yet the truth of these behind-the-scenes events remains necessarily veiled and only partially explained. Does Nastasya Filippovna remain "apart" when with Rogozhin? Does she truly shame him with an officer, as Rogozhin charges, or is it that whatever transpired was done for show alone to fuel further his volatile imagination? Of far greater importance, however, is the problem of whether Nastasya Filippovna is closer to Myshkin's compassionate, idealized image of her (seized upon initially and crystallized solely by the impression her portrait first makes upon him) or to Rogozhin's demoniac vision of her derived from his unfulfilled desire. For Myshkin, she is tortured; this he perceives with his love which is not love. For Rogozhin, she is torturer; this he feels with a love which is pain. Through compassion Myshkin can project her hurt; Rogozhin feels nothing but his own. As a result of such tensions, generated from within and without the plot (by means of the "told account"), the reader is left intrigued, groping for the psychological truth behind the character's actions—behind what is shown and what is not.

The Idiot is a novel of intrigues pyramided one upon another. However, not all of these are dramatized as part of the novel's developed sequence of events. A singular technique by which the diegetic mode is effected, as opposed to the dramatic, may be registered at those critical moments when the characters of the novel are thrust on stage, as it were, to assume predetermined postures, resulting from antecedent situations that are only later explained. When Myshkin first visits Rogozhin, for instance, the latter is at first struck dumb at the sight of him, causing Myshkin as well belated consternation. But the reader is initially left uninformed as to the cause of their mutual discomfiture—that Nastasya Filippovna had been alternately seeking safety from the one in the other—since that information is elicited only from what little is made evident in the dialogue between them. In numerous other such instances, the characters burst in upon one another from behind what one might assume to be closed doors—but which, as a basic convention of the Dostoevsky novel, never are. Thus they appear en masse at Ganya's, at Nastasya Filippovna's, and at Myshkin's. On each occasion, the effect is one of surprise and shock at the sudden appearance of unexpected guests—one or more of whom will inevitably make demands that elicit detailed explanations of prior events. These, in turn, are eventually followed by a general clamor and riotous behavior, ending in scandal. One such instance is the Burdovsky affair.

When the callow, inexperienced Burdovsky appears falsely to lay claim as the "son of Pavlishchev" to a share of Myshkin's inheritance, certain characters are ostensibly informed to varying degrees of the awkward situation; however, the reader is not. The format of these scenes (II, 8-10), when everything comes to light, is set at Lebedyev's dacha, where numerous disparate individuals have gathered, as Myshkin convalesces after an epileptic attack. Onto this already less than tranquil scene appear four young men requiring an immediate audience with the prince in order to demand "their rights." Following their entrance, the young Kolya Ivolgin, an admirer of the prince, is requested to read a crude newspaper article—amounting, in effect, to a distorted descriptive report—designed to humiliate Myshkin. Amidst the uproar that follows, the prince comments on the situation—as the account is brought into sharper focus—by explaining what the claim amounts to and what has been done so far to satisfy it. Finally, as Myshkin's appointed agent, Ganya picks up the story where the prince leaves off to sketch in the third panel of this diegetic triptych, by supplying the final crushing details that ultimately rout the unfortunate claimants.[4]

Such is the skeletal framework of the scene which now makes the reader privy to information which had previously been withheld. The ungainly youths' unexpected arrival and awkward departure are orchestrated outside the reader's purview. Hence this dramatized scene represents the "effects" of backstage "causes," whose hidden design is made evident through the juxtaposition of oddly complementary recapitulations of hitherto unknown events. Both the trumped-up charges and the eventual resolution to the problem are thus *reported* to the reader, in both instances, after the fact, while only the resultant series of outcries and subsequent humiliations are explicitly *dramatized* as part of the plot proper. In this essentially formulaic manner, the vigor and excitement of the Dostoevskian *skandal* is consistently effected.

Affording an additional summative recapitulation, Mme. Epanchina, in a paroxysm of anger, immediately reconstructs the events just enacted, casting blame on Burdovsky and com-

pany for their cheap mercenariness disguised behind a vague
set of distorted ideals, and on Myshkin as well for his perceived
perverse desire not only to forgive his tormentors but also
lavish an undeserved reward upon them as misguided compensation. As a result of her angry reconstruction of events, the
plot moves on to a new concern: the pathetic figure of the
perversely gifted, dying adolescent, as Ippolit takes the central
place in the novel, where his story reaches its apogee in his
failed suicide attempt.

The scenes during which Ippolit attains the central place
(III, 5-7) may also illustrate further the basic interplay in the
novel between the descriptive report and its correspondent
dramatized sequence of events. The episode begins with the
drama of much vigorous debate—over the meaning of the
Apocalypse, the problem of man's opposed instincts for both
self-preservation and self-destruction, the existence of the
devil, a unique instance of cannibalism, and sundry other topics
raised seemingly spontaneously in the heat of the moment and
dropped just as quickly. By contrast to all the attendant
histrionics, which make the scene dramatic in one sense, Ippolit
uncertainly takes the floor to read his "Essential Explanation,"
which leads to further dramatic consequence. Gradually, the
multiplicity of fragmented dialogue yields to monologue, as the
clamor of voices is replaced by a single adolescent's lonely cry
for sympathy and understanding. Itself a striking instance of an
extended descriptive report, Ippolit's "confession" documents
its author's tortuous psychological path, concluding in the
recognition that suicide represents an acceptable alternative to
his sad plight. As another occasion when the one prototypical
form of narrative discourse may be seen logically to replace the
other, Ippolit's desperate suicide attempt marks the tumul-
tuous conclusion to the scene, when the deed—emanating from
the articulated word—again ultimately supersedes its verbal
formulation, allowing for the two interwoven narrative modes
consistently to serve the book's unifying, integrative ends.

Toward the close of the novel (IV, 8-10), among the flurry of visitors who come to see Myshkin after he has suffered an attack (following the fiasco with the vase), Ippolit appears, spiteful and malicious, seemingly breathing his last—and brimming with information concerning two unexpected meetings. The first, between Ganya and Aglaya, has already taken place; the other, between Aglaya and Nastasya Filippovna, has yet to occur. Myshkin is astounded at the news.

> Hey, are you really unaware that Aglaya Ivanovna is going to meet Nastasya Filippovna today? And that for that purpose Nastasya Filippovna has been brought, through Rogozhin, from Petersburg, at an invitation of Aglaya Ivanovna and by my efforts, is now staying with Rogozhin, where she stayed before, very near you, in the house of that woman . . . Darya Alexeyevna . . . a very dubious lady, a friend of hers, and to that very doubtful house Aglaya Ivanovna is going today to have a friendly conversation with Nastasya Filippovna, and to decide various problems. They want to work at arithmetic. Didn't you know it? Honour bright? (545-46)

Thus Myshkin (and the reader) are again brought up to date on affairs that take place on another episodic plane. But since they bear directly on the subsequent course of events, they need first to be explained. And to fulfill that informative, preparatory role, Ippolit leaves his sickbed one last time. Afterwards, all that remains is for the two women of the novel to have their climactic meeting, when the remote possibility of further dialogue and all hope of mutual understanding are irreparably sundered.

Their talk is initiated in silence, as each takes careful measure of the other. Yet, in complementing their expressive features, the silence itself again proves communicative, as the moments of non-verbal communication attain their inevitable

result: "At last she looked resolutely straight into Nastasya
Filippovna's face and read at once all that was revealed in the
ominous gleam in her rival's eyes. Woman understood woman"
(549). The verbal duel that ensues begins with a calculated
series of probes designed to expose one another's vulnerability.
Aglaya's brief, unexpected monologue ("Hear my answer to all
your letters." 550), however, almost immediately takes precedence, followed by her blatantly declaring to her rival her love
for a man whom she had allowed all others—including her
family and Myshkin himself—to think she despises. Thus, at
the start, anger and recrimination give way, as she allows her
heart, during a single, unguarded moment, to have its say. "I
have to tell you, too, that I have never in my life met a man like
him for noble simplicity, and boundless trustfulness. I understood from the way he talked that anyone who chose could
deceive him, and that he would forgive anyone afterwards who
had deceived him, and that was why I grew to love him . . ."
(551). Affording psychological insight and the posture of an
immediately regretted confessional attitude, monologic statement preempts dialogic discourse, with the former embedded,
as it were, in the latter. Moreover, in this instance as well, the
diegetic mode achieves precedence, when what was veiled and
implicit is made irrefutably explicit. That Aglaya's "confession"
is pivotal in the two women's talk becomes clearly evident,
since it foments the vengeful, wrathful turn of events by which
first the one woman, out of pride, and then the other, for the
same reason, regrets her moment of openness and decency, and
irrevocably changes course, assuring the impossibility of any
further rapprochement.

   Paralleling Ippolit's previous account of undramatized
events, and serving essentially the same reportive function,
authorial accounts, characterized by vagueness and uncertainty, are variously presented as the planned marriage between
Myshkin and Nastasya Filippovna is considered from numerous
perspectives (IV, 9). Perverse and distorted, the views of the

townspeople, for instance, are projected as an exaggerated blend of speculation and suspicion complimentary to neither the prospective bride nor groom. Further, all purported summations by an authorial voice are continually reduced to bare suppositions ("because we find it difficult in many instances to explain what occurred" 556). A complex array of intentionally uncertain reports is thus presented with no conclusive account rendered.

> We can only say one thing, that the marriage really was arranged . . . that Nastasya Filippovna was insisting on the wedding and in haste for it . . . that the wedding day had been fixed for the beginning of July . . .that Nastasya Filippovna certainly did desire a speedy wedding, and that it was she, and not Myshkin, who had thought of the wedding. Thus, we know for a fact that during that fortnight Myshkin spent whole days and evenings with Nastasya Filippovna; that she took him with her for walks and to hear the band, that he drove out in her carriage with her every day; that he began to be uneasy about her if an hour passed without seeing her . . . that whatever she talked to him about, he listened with a mild and gentle smile for hours together, saying scarcely anything himself. (558-59)

Such vague, extended reports thus temporarily supersede dramatic presentation. Similarly, in the following chapter, the central place is devoted to an account of Myshkin and Nastasya Filippovna, in which, again characteristically, virtually none of their moments together is set forth as drama. Instead, the reader is informed of specific incidents which take place between them, suggestive of the woman's deteriorating mental state. Thus it is reported that "her melancholy and brooding grew more marked every hour," making it increasingly clear that "the poor soul had broken down" (573). Only once is a single piece of direct speech incorporated into the account, accompanied by a dramatic gesture, itself as communicative as the words simultaneously uttered.

> "What am I doing? What am I doing? What am I doing
> to you?" she cried, embracing his feet convulsively.
> (575)

It is only left now for the "mad woman" to take cognizance of her own desperate words, abort the wedding scene, and seek instead refuge, salvation, and obliteration in the haunting figure of Rogozhin.

The book's concluding chapter details Myshkin's search for the devastated woman. In counterpoint to the preceding passages discussed—and to the novel as a whole, where detailed explanation and report frequently subsume dramatic interaction and attendant dialogue—the chapter depicting the climactic denouement is rendered in contrastive but similarly compelling manner. During the terrible process of search and discovery no further accounts are either rendered or forthcoming. Monologic discourse yields exclusively to dialogic; diegetic account to mimetic; while all that precedes—from Myshkin's first hearing of Nastasya Filippovna on the train arriving to St. Petersburg, to his coincidentally seeing her picture and being confronted by the woman herself that same day, and then all that follows—serves as the fitting preparation for that driving momentum which culminates in the seemingly inevitable end. Now there is logically and conclusively nothing left to tell; all previously detailed causes have achieved their one awesome dramatized effect. The triangle of misplaced compassion, murderous obsession, and suicidal despair has at long last been precluded from all further human relations which, as the book has implied all along, and as the technique here outlined has served to confirm, endure finally and conclusively as mystery.

*

In the preceding discussion, the concept of monologue is implicitly associated (but not equated) with that of descriptive report, while dialogue is conceived as a potential constituent of a work's narrative chain of dramatized events. The descriptive report, virtually by definition, is monologic in form (presuming no interruption by another speaker), although it may be embedded within a greater encompassing dialogue; likewise, dialogue itself is encompassed within a novel's dramatized sequence of events, at times as a distinctively dramatic feature, especially in the case of Dostoevsky. What links the preceding discussion to what follows in this chapter is the clear relation that exists between the descriptive report and reported speech. First, both are past oriented in an effort to render an account of what has already occurred beyond the reader's purview, in order to prepare for what is yet to take place. Second, these are joint endeavors in the sense that reported speech is often embedded within the descriptive report. Our focus will therefore shift to consider the problem of reported speech from the perspective of its role within a centrally important past. To accommodate this perspective, we shift as well from Dostoevsky's second major novel to his third.

Although Stavrogin is the author of various philosophical arguments and political strategies, he never expresses his own ideas. Rather, they are articulated only by advocates desperate to light upon a soul-saving philosophy or upon a nihilistic mode of political action. In the absence of direct speech on the part of the hero, his long discarded past views are expressed by a series of disciples as reported speech. Paradoxically, that speech takes on a certain authoritative aura for the character articulating it, which it did not have for its original speaker, who had been experimenting with a number of mutually opposed philosophies. Stavrogin's original thought may thus be understood as a form of discourse that is inherently inconclusive and therefore open to further modification, as opposed to an authoritative mode of discourse that brooks no dispute or further dialogic response. While the author's theory had been open and inconclusive (his unwillingness to subscribe ultimately to any one view demonstrates the point), his word had been appropriated by various characters as final and correct. In a word, as Truth.

The problem of the appropriation of one speaker's discourse by another, who may employ it in a manner either directly or obliquely opposed to the original intention, is fundamental to *The Possessed*. Most strikingly, Shatov, Kirillov, and Petr Verkhovensky all appropriate Stavrogin's word (in its varied and contradictory manifestations) as their own guiding philosophy for reasons that are personal, psychological, and political—but that differ radically from Stavrogin's own present (and presumably past) apprehensions of his own utterances. Pertinent to the problem of reported speech in general and to its employment in this novel in particular are the interrelated questions of *who* is employing another's word? For what purpose and in what manner? And is this (present) purpose and manner in basic accord with that of the original speaker's perceived intent, or not? What the reader must come to grips with in this work is that the hero's word is consistently employed in a manner that ultimately runs contrary to its original hypothetical posture. As a result, Stavrogin's teachings as reported speech become authoritative for each respective adherent. Notwithstanding its total absence from the text, Stavrogin's direct speech, it may be surmised, is consistently taken out of its original unfinalized context and pronounced instead as conclusive and convincing.

How Stavrogin's programmatic thinking is communicated to the reader, within several critical passages, will constitute the present concern. Accordingly, it will be implicitly argued, in conformity with our previously noted positive attribution, that the novel is largely governed by a poetics of absence that nevertheless inspires in the reader a felt presence. Regarding *The Idiot*, the focus had been primarily on the event left un-dramatized (for whatever thematic purpose); by contrast, here we will concentrate instead on the word left unsaid (by its original author). *The Possessed* also achieves its ends, however, by strategic omission on various levels. To illustrate briefly the point, an immediate, all-pervasive compositional principle at work in *The Idiot* may be contrasted to the later novel. In the earlier work, Myshkin is clearly central to the whole ideational conception of the novel. But, as affirmed by Mochulsky, the centrality of Stavrogin in the latter also appears irrefutable: "in fact, the whole novel is the fate of Stavrogin alone, everything is about him and everything is for him" (1971:434).

While this assessment meets with general concensus, the hero is paradoxically absent for long, extended passages in the book. In part one, which covers more than 150 pages, Stavrogin appears briefly in just a few of those pages: as the perpetrator of scandal, the instigator of duels, as "murderer" of an op-ponent, the subject of numerous and varied innuendos, and participant in debauchery in the lowest haunts of Petersburg—all of which, significantly, takes place in the past. He is absent in the introductory chapter, appears as "Prince Harry" in the second, and is referred to obliquely in the third ("The Sins of Others"). Stavrogin's name is mentioned only once in chapter four (by Shatov, who acknowledges him as the man who sent a hundred rubles for his passage home from America). Finally, he appears in the novel's present in the fifth and concluding chapter of part one. Of the ten chapters of part two, Stavrogin does not appear in chapters four, five, nine and ten, and makes only a brief appearance at the end of six. Of the eight chapters of part three, he is present only in the third and eighth. In *The Idiot*, by contrast, the protagonist appears in virtually every scene.

Yet, as an equally significant contrastive convention of that novel, the reader must accept the notion that there could ever have been such a figure as Prince Myshkin in the first place. If that basic supposition were to be regarded as untenable or unbelievable, the novel would most likely prove unreadable. The concept of a *yurodivy* prince, in other words, represents a possibility in the actual world (of nineteenth-century Russia), which, when transferred to the world of fiction, constitutes a purely literary convention that in the one work is paramount. In the other, however, the reader must likewise accept as believable a contrastive demonic prince, incarnate in Stavrogin, who is both central to that work and yet largely absent from it.

Each individual novel, then, ultimately establishes its own set of conventions or individual poetics. Yet, within the broad, distinctive lineaments of various novels, there are bound to be points of coincidence. Thus, in accord with *The Idiot*, and perhaps exceeding it in this respect, events in *The Possessed* that are not dramatized also attain a seemingly disproportionate prominence. Stavrogin's vital period of experimentation, his God-seeking and period of debauchery, as related instances, have all taken place in the past—prior to the opening moments of the novel—and consistently remain undepicted and unshown, though very much known. Likewise, the manner by which the novel's chronicler provides information is frequently cryptic, appearing at times more dissimulative than communicative. Hence the hallmark statement: "It was a day of surprises, a day that solved past riddles and suggested new ones, a day of startling revelations, and still more hopeless perplexity" (168).

There is a whole series of occurrences in *The Possessed*, as frequently remarked, to which the reader is made privy in an intentionally obscure manner. Occurring in another time and place from the novel's main time frame, such off-stage events include Stavrogin's reported duels, his relations with Liza and Darya respectively, his financial dealings with the captain and marriage to the latter's sister, and his earlier associations with Shatov, Kirillov, and Petr Verkhovensky. These interrelated episodes, among others, contribute to the novel's structure as a "temporal palimpsest" (Holquist 1977:130), an impression which is further enhanced by Stavrogin's disappearance (after perpetrating a series of scandals) for more than a hundred pages—and four years of novelistic time. Moreover, this exceptional absence, in accord with the novel's governing poetics, determines not only the hero's extended temporal and spatial displacement but also, paradoxically, his centrality.

In assessing problems of novelistic time and the related concept of what constitutes a work's "fictive present," one theorist designates its opening temporal boundary as being the first "time section" that the narrator finds important enough "to deserve full scenic treatment, and turns it, implicitly but clearly, into a conspicuous signpost, signifying that this is precisely the point in time that the author has decided . . . to make the reader regard as the beginning of the action proper" (Sternberg 1978:20). In *The Possessed* that "signpost" is explicitly demarcated as follows by the erstwhile chronicler: "I will now enter upon the description of that almost forgotten incident with which my story properly speaking begins" (83). Thus is the fictive present inaugurated some fifty pages into the work, making the two opening chapters analeptic, in Genette's terms, or past-oriented, in one sense, but at the same time anticipatory of later events. In selectively presenting only certain peculiar episodes from the past to relate as requisite background information, the first two chapters are designed to provide a tension-filled framework for understanding the present, and thus serve as the designated pretext for the story that follows.

Within the primary time frame of the present, the appearance of the work's central character is significantly delayed until that moment set in the crowded drawing room of Mme. Stavrogina, when, well into the novel, Petr Verkhovensky heralds his entrance, as though announcing the drama's star performer. ". . . Ah, here's Nikolai Vsevolodovich; keep quiet please" (199). However, the moment is short-lived but crucial, as Stavrogin enters the room, obliquely denies his mother's immediate question as to whether Marya Timofeevna is his wife, and addresses instead the submissive young woman wishing to kneel before him. "Only think that you are a girl, and that though I'm your devoted friend I'm an outsider, not your husband, nor your father, nor your betrothed" (201). On that false note, they exit; the hero, magnetic and imperious, with the cripple hobbling alongside, fearfully inept and ashamed—only not for herself, but for him. For essentially with his first utterance Stavrogin gives the lie, in response to which the young woman departs in silence, and Shatov later strikes him in silence. In the hero's absence, however, Petr Verkhovensky remains to break the silence and tell the story, by weaving a pattern of both truth and lie, as he relates Stavrogin's exploits in Petersburg five years past.

Throughout Verkhovensky's expansive account of the years of card-playing, carousing, and debauchery, he cites only a single statement (regarding Marya Timofeevna) directly attributed to Stavrogin: "You imagine . . . that I am laughing at her. Get rid of that idea. I really do respect her, for she is better than any of us" (205). His extended account is immediately followed by the anxious recapitulation of Varvara Petrovna, inspired by that single instance of reported speech, which the mother hastens to interpret as an index of her son's "loftiness of soul" and "sacred" concern for "a creature ill-treated by everyone, crippled, half-insane, and at the same time perhaps filled with noble feelings" (207). Stavrogin's single putative utterance, within Verkhovensky's relatively lengthy account, serves as the sole source for the woman's interpretation and explanation of her son's paradoxical behavior. Everything can be made right, presumably, if one only takes cognizance of and correctly interprets Stavrogin's words. This is the underlying premise that motivates the mother. It is also the model for the hermeneutic upon which the entire novel is based. Virtually every character in the book takes the same misguided ap-

proach: if one can only get the Word from Stavrogin and interpret it correctly, one will attain the truth and an instructive
philosophy.

So Stavrogin initially articulates the lie; Verkhovensky expands upon it; Varvara Petrovna gives credence to it; while the
sorry figure of the captain is made in turn to confirm it. The
importance of such undermining of the truth is underscored by
the fact that the entire novel turns on what is fundamentally
untrue: that Stavrogin is still possessed of a dynamism and will
that can provide an answer to the vicissitudes of life. Only the
demented cripple recognizes the truth by distinguishing between the "you" of the present and the "him" of the past when
addressing Stavrogin directly (294-95). In addition, one need
only recall the earlier passage where Varvara Petrovna perceives her son as a lifeless corpse and recoils in horror (247).
That is the image which most truthfully and most awfully
reflects the character's spiritually moribund state. But in part
that general false impression of retained vitality is sustained,
simply, by the hero's absence from the scene. What the reader
has to go on, in other words, parallels the situation of the
mother in the dramatic instance just cited, and that of the other
characters as well in related instances. It is not so much what
we are given to "see" as to "hear," since Stavrogin's exploits are
for the most part not dramatized as present event but related
as past incident.

Thus within the given conclave scene, Varvara Petrovna's
detailed response to the story related by Petr Verkhovensky is
evoked specifically by those words purportedly belonging to her
son. Embedded within the past-oriented account, that significant isolated piece of reported speech is further embedded within the dramatic events detailed during the present conclave.
Yet from within that series of superimposed verbal constructs,
Stavrogin's reported utterance is projected onto the plane of
current concerns. Achieving prominence as a result, the repeated articulation (Petr Verkhovensky, Varvara Petrovna) of

what might have seemed an insignificant remark reflects in microcosm the ideational conception of the novel as a whole: articulated in the past, Stavrogin's words retain a certain flickering vitality for others, but have long been extinguished in the mind of their author.

From one perspective, as noted, reported speech may be viewed as a reconstruction of a past utterance that potentially affords vital present significance, when incorporated within a new dialogical context. Contrary to this viable theoretical standpoint, although Stavrogin's utterances are reaffirmed by various disciples, affording a renewed "hearing" in a necessarily different context, they are essentially deprived of their original significance by their author's current rejection of them. The story itself, on the other hand, as told in the course of this one scene, effectively dramatizes the power of the incorporated tale. Yet, as the disturbing correlative upon which much of the novel turns, what is also dramatized is the power of the lie. Superimposed within Dostoevsky's fiction, his characters' fictions are thus initially and fundamentally misconstrued, but are in this novel consistently taken as truth.

As a case in point, when Petr Verkhovensky grills the captain regarding the account he has just rendered of Stavrogin's Petersburg period and of his relationship to Marya Timofeevna, he asks:

> . . . is it *all* true that I've said?
> It is true.
>
> . . . .
> Is it *all* true?
> It's all true. (211)

Notwithstanding the captain's affirmation, it is of course not *all* true. And yet, Varvara Petrovna enthusiastically accepts it as such.

With far greater perspecuity, Stavrogin observes upon his return with regard to Petr Verkhovensky: "He's such a realist, you know, that he can't tell a lie, and prefers truthfulness to effect . . . except, of course, in special cases when effect is more important than truth" (213). Clearly, such a "special case" has just transpired.

Stavrogin rarely speaks of his past. (He makes an exception when he informs Shatov that he is in fact married.) Instead, the chronicler and Verkhovensky, offering the reader a few hints and the bare lineaments of the hero's biography, provide the necessary information. Similarly, Stavrogin himself never articulates his own ideas, nor does any authorial voice serve to redress the balance. The one exception is the expurgated chapter, "At Tikhon's," which, in affording Stavrogin his own voice, as it were, contrasts greatly—as has been frequently remarked—with the rest of the work. This obvious lacuna is thus only partially compensated for by Stavrogin's series of interlocutors (Shatov, Kirillov, Verkhovensky) who, in highly truncated, abbreviated fashion, outline a series of significantly differing philosophies that have evidently been short-lived. Each acknowledges the important role Stavrogin as ideologist has played in the past, but their shared sentiment is also wrongly projected into the future, as Shatov heatedly declares as seeming spokesman for virtually every character in the novel: "You, only you can raise that flag!" (271).

In alternating dialogue with the two former visitors to America, Stavrogin is obliged to serve as unwilling audience as his own diametrically opposed ideas (that man must become his own god; that man must have faith in some being greater than himself) are fervently reformulated by his former disciples, who are seeking current validation by their author for outworn ideologies. In neither case, significantly, does the master add anything new. Although now articulated by others, Stavrogin's teachings, presented as reported speech, in effect model the structure of the work as a whole, where the hero—as a potential source of further instruction—has nothing more to say. What had been taken essentially at face value as authoritative speech in the past (but, again, not necessarily projected as such initially) is diminished in the present, since the one voice has been replaced by a series of far less convincing ones.

From a related perspective, the internal dynamics differentiating the original level of discourse from its reenactment as fervently reported speech may be further explored in terms outlined by Bakhtin, who distinguishes briefly between what he terms "the internally persuasive word" as opposed to "the authoritative word" (1981:346). The former represents an open expression of ideas seeking a response in the search for philosophic truth. Articulated by a speaker already convinced of his ideology, the latter is closed off to further dialogue and possible dissent. When Stavrogin initially expresses his ideas, inculcating others with opposing but convincing viewpoints, he is, in effect, articulating an internally persuasive discourse, as he attempts to persuade himself perhaps most of all (as he confesses to Shatov) of the veracity of *some* point of view. However, when these same viewpoints are later uttered by the hero's disciples (in the novel's present), they appear as authoritative discourse—having been originally apprehended as such—characterized by the new adherents' conviction of their absolute truthfulness. Significantly, in this respect as well, the truth-seekers in the novel (excluding Stavrogin) are taken in by another fiction—the notion that any single individual alone bears an ultimate truth.

As reported speech, and in the terms just outlined, Stavrogin's ideas are thus transformed from open, dialogically accented modes of discourse to closed, monologically intoned speech. When Stavrogin initially expresses his series of contradictory ideas, they are implicitly open, we may assume, to further argumentation and assessment. When his students rearticulate the same set of philosophical notions, they are convinced of their rightness, although their original author is not. Kirillov, for instance, informs the erstwhile chronicler:

> Now man is not yet what he will be. There will be a new man, happy and proud. For whom it will be the same to live or not to live, he will be the new man. He who will conquer pain and terror will himself be a god. And this God will not be. He who kills himself only to kill fear will become a god at once. (133,134)

Similarly (but in contradictory terms), Shatov informs Stavrogin:

> But there is only one truth, and therefore only a single one out of the nations can have the true God, even though other nations may have great gods of their own. Only one nation is 'god-bearing,' that's the Russian people. (269)

In this nondisputational manner, Stavrogin's teachings are not subjected to further analysis, nor to some form of philosophical confrontation. Rather, his words—as the words of the "other" (*čužaja reč'*, reported speech, literally rendered)[5]—are unequivocally adopted by the new advocate as his convinced unassailable stand. On this significant count alone, such a position differs profoundly from that originally taken. Earlier Stavrogin's words were offered as a conceivably viable personal or political ideology; now they are taken as truth. The responsibility for their original "implantation" belongs to the author of these contending ideas, but for their eventual transformation (and unwanted elevation) one must look to his disciples.

Thus when Shatov observes to Stavrogin: "These are your own words, Stavrogin . . . I haven't altered anything of your ideas or even of your words, not a syllable," the latter retorts: "I don't agree that you've not altered anything . . . You accepted them with ardor, and in your ardor have transformed them unconsciously" (268). That observation, in effect, encapsulates the present amounts to a shift from the original author's open, hypothetical stance to its appropriation as authoritative speech. Shatov therefore demands that Stavrogin acknowledge the underlying authority of his own words. But throughout their talk the latter consistently refuses to do so.

The author of these ideas not only refuses to express or reformulate his views, but appears to reject implicitly what others enthusiastically accept. Just as the hero's voice is not heard on the level of biography, likewise on the plane of political ideology Stavrogin does not articulate the ideas attributed to him. These are presented, however, as only minimally formulated—or consistently fragmented—by the voice of some other, whose own articulation is only weakly reminiscent of that originating voice strenuously in dialogue with itself, but now grown indifferent. Thus Verkhovensky affirms after the abortive political meeting: "But you wrote the rules yourself, there's no need to explain" (403). And, in seeming authorial conformity with this fictive guiding dictum, the entire political underpinning of what is deemed by common consensus "Dostoevsky's political novel" remains almost exclusively implicit. As an exception, the work's active political architect makes explicit what will never be realized: "You and I," Verkhovensky says to Stavrogin, "are the central committee and there will be as many branches as we like" (403). From that single belated cryptic remark the reader must generate for himself the entire complex framework upon which the abortive meeting itself and the projected relations of its misguided participants are founded.

But during that same seminal talk, in complementary fashion, Stavrogin suggests to Verkhovensky (clearly not for the first time), as an even more haunting, cryptic remark—"persuade four members of the circle to do for a fifth" (404)—thus grounding the political denouement of the work in a single sinister idea irrefutably belonging to Stavrogin as author. Hence the observation that "you wrote the rules yourself," affirmed by Verkhovensky, is immediately confirmed by Stavrogin's own singular programmatic statement. But never does he go beyond this, in a single instance, to explicate or elaborate. And neither do his disciples in their extended dialogues with him. Verkhovensky's further remark, "there's no need to explain," therefore also seems programmatic. But this stricture, oddly, appears applicable to the composition of the text itself. For on the level of biography, the reader is treated to a host of rumors and innuendo, and on that of ideology, analogously, to the hero's discordant visions presented in fragmentary form by disciples who want them revalidated by their now disillusioned author.

In sum, these "visions" amount to a total of four principal ideas in the book, all attributed—explicitly or implicitly—to Stavrogin. The first two, briefly formulated and adopted by Kirillov and Shatov respectively, may be expressed as that of man aspiring to be God as opposed to that of man seeking God. Both are significant in the characterization of their respective principal exponents, but more so, in the paradoxical depiction of their author, who is ostensibly capable of expounding and inculcating the two contradictory notions in others simultaneously. Also attributed to Stavrogin, the third principal idea, that blood might serve as the most effective binding agent of a small political cell, is the diabolical pivot upon which the political plot of the novel turns and its eventual denouement depends. However, unlike *Crime and Punishment* and *The Brothers Karamazov*, where Raskolnikov in the one novel and Ivan Karamazov in the other wrestle with essentially the same governing concept (that a self-proclaimed superior individual may allow himself dispensation to commit a crime in the name of some "ideal"), in this novel the protagonist engages in no such *agon*. Rather, he is no longer challenged by his own ideas, nor by any others. By extinguishing in the hero the capacity for spiritual struggle, the potential for life is likewise negated. In abstract reformulation, Stavrogin's ideas—as expressed in the novel's present—represent independent monologic statement hopelessly excluded from the possibility of dialogic integration.

In that sense, when Bakhtin observes that "In *The Possessed*, there is not a single idea that fails to find a dialogic response in Stavrogin's consciousness" (1984:73), his remark appears insufficient to the novel on two counts. First, essentially all of the ideas expressed in the book belong to Stavrogin initially as their original author, which makes the observation oddly tautological. Conversely, none of those ideas, when articulated for his subsequent approval (in the novel's present), manages to evoke from him a single resonant note. There is, then, no "dialogic response in Stavrogin's consciousness" to his own earlier expressed ideas, nor do they find such dialogic responsiveness elsewhere—in the macrocosmic community (reflective of the hero's closed-off consciousness), where, representing their ultimate ramifications, the master's teachings are effected finally and monologically as suicide and murder.

Moreover, the presentation of the novel's ideas—articulated exclusively by a series of despondent adherents in fragmented, unintegrated fashion—is itself designed to model the disintegrative, fragmentary nature of an ideology no longer espoused by its originator. The hero's initial statements, in other words, ultimately taken as authoritative and monologic, are not incorporated within some form of dialogic communication. They remain instead isolated fragments, just as those who espouse their various contradictory formulations are similarly cut off from human community. The discordance on the plane of ideology therefore reflects a similar disharmony on the level of social relations.

The fourth idea, espousing a political program that nine-tenths of society be enslaved to a superior one-tenth, which would guarantee the happiness and well-being of the majority, is ostensibly attributed to the awkward Shigalov. However, it appears implicitly as yet another idea belonging originally to Stavrogin. This may be argued from several interrelated viewpoints. First, as obvious instances of reported speech, the ideas espoused by Shatov and Kirillov, respectively, are explicitly attributed to Stavrogin by their current advocates. Similarly, Petr Verkhovensky firmly declares that Stavrogin himself had prescribed the sinister machinations upon which the political plot depends. As a perhaps less explicit form of report (immediately substantiated, however, by Stavrogin, as shown), it is one which nevertheless goes some way towards making the case: namely, that Stavrogin's words—as both explicit reported speech and implicitly as his ideas—appear to extend beyond any formal "frame" that might otherwise afford a certain border to a given instance of reported speech. Rather, Stavrogin's words are not framed; there are no borders—or, better, his putative utterances overflow whatever borders might normally pertain.

This same idea may be expressed by drawing upon Bakhtin's abstract notion of "character zone," expressed thus: "A character in a novel always has . . . a zone of his own, his own sphere of influence on the authorial context surrounding him, a sphere that extends—and often quite far—beyond the boundaries of the direct discourse allotted to him. The area occupied by an important character's voice must in any event be broader than his direct and 'actual' words" (1981:320). The case of Stavrogin illustrates the point. His "character zone" embraces the entire ideological plane of the novel. It is in this sense, moreover, that one might apply or extend Mochulsky's earlier cited insistence upon Stavrogin's centrality. As a definitive feature of the novel's individual poetics, one need not isolate an idea ("Shigalov's," for example) as being specifically attributable to Stavrogin. Ultimately, his "zone" appears so expansive as to encompass—in explicit or implicit terms—all of the programmatic ideas expressed in the work.

With the presentation of this last idea as well, the same basic structural pattern novel is reaffirmed. That is, the idea is initially articulated in brief (by the lame school teacher present at the meeting), and is then later expounded in greater detail (by Petr Verkhovensky). But its author (whether presumed to be Shigalov or originally Stavrogin) never explicates, nor elaborates. In this final instance, too, the idea is never given its original expression but appears instead as (several times removed) reported speech. Yet, as in the other instances noted, it is also regarded as authoritative and final by the hero's disciples who, if not seeking further development or elaboration, want at least some reconfirmation. And this is not forthcoming.

Stavrogin's words, moreover, are diametrically opposed to one another (Shatov and Kirillov), and therefore preclude the related possibility of further "internal" debate. Their fragmentary, oppositional nature, in other words, does not evoke a sense of their potential or eventual cohesion: the binding of individuals through crime might assist, in theory, in the formation of small political cells, but neither such consideration bears any explicit relation to those other (man-god or god-man) theories, which belong more to a philosophical-spiritual plane than to Verkhovensky's active political campaign. Similarly discordant, Shatov's god-seeking and the notion of "Shigalovism" find no corresponding thematic development to their ideational expression. Yet as fragments of an inconsistent, contradictory ideology which never seeks, it would seem, their eventual integration, that evident lack also serves to reflect further upon the complementary fragmented quality of their author-ideologist and his resultant, ultimate capitulation.

In a novel where the main ideological viewpoints are consistently expressed as reported speech, Petr Verkhovensky's assessment of Stavrogin's "extraordinary aptitude for crime" (271) is cited at one point by Stavrogin himself. What that assessment might mean deserves brief concluding consideration. On one level, as a kind of requisite, it neatly corresponds to Petr Verkhovensky's perverted view of what it takes to initiate political action. (As Stavrogin also notes tellingly, he reportedly views him as the Stenka Razin of the "movement"). At the same time that assessment may be understood as the reasonable response to a mind that conceives of blood as an effective binding agent in blatant recognition of "political necessity." But it may also be interpreted as the protagonist's disturbing ability to remain unaffected by the working out of his theories in practice: Kirillov's suicide, Shatov's murder. And, in this sense, that view of the novel's protagonist (as cited by him no less) appears to encapsulate the criminally indifferent attitude of an individual who is unwilling to take responsibility for the ramifications of his own conflicting theories, as cited by others.

4

Dialogic Structures

Crime and Punishment

Throughout the second half of Dostoevsky's first major novel, a series of dialogues between Sonya and Raskolnikov alternate with a second series between the latter and Porfiry Petrovich. Treated earlier from the perspective of the nonverbal strategies they encompass, it remains to consider them now from their dominant verbal aspect. At one point these talks are consecutive; Raskolnikov leaves Sonya late at night, after their first meeting (IV:4), and goes to Porfiry the next morning for their second (IV:5-6). Essentially, these six interconnected dialogues attempt to account for several related truths: first, the problem of who committed the crime (a fact which Raskolnikov needs to convey to Sonya, but which Porfiry must hear from Raskolnikov); second, why it was committed—a question which both the former student and detective attempt to resolve within their respective contextual frameworks. Raskolnikov seeks out Sonya, whose role remains passive and forgiving; Porfiry actively seeks a confession by means of a strategy which requires that it be outlined in detail for its targeted quarry, whose eventual complicity is needed for it to succeed. Porfiry, we may assume, knows who committed the crime; hence the dialogue between him and its perpetrator serves as a medium through which the problems of *who* and *why* are explored. Raskolnikov, it might be presumed, would know (surely within the framework of a lesser novel) why it was committed, and yet, in complementary fashion, his dialogue with Sonya serves as a related medium through which he himself explores that very problem. In brief, these alternating dialogues represent in their totality structures of necessarily complex discourse that attempt to account for a truth, which may nevertheless appear ultimately, if not conclusively, disparate and fragmented.

Articulated in the present by one or more speakers, dialogue does not take place outside of time but within it, taking full cognizance of past utterances and of possible future ones as well. As a direct result of its taking such cognizance, the problem of reported speech inevitably emerges as a principal concern. As Bakhtin stresses with regard to both literary and quotidian discourse: "The problem of the artistic representation of another's speech . . . is the central problem of novelistic prose . . . .The transmission and assessment of the speech of others, the discourse of another, is one of the most widespread and fundamental topics of human speech . . ." In addition, he declares discourse as the subject of discourse "a subject *sui generis* . . . " (1981:337). In this chapter, that crucial *sui generis* subject will be accommodated by three possible formats, serving as model, within whose joint domain the problem of reported speech may be provisionally contained. These include what will here be termed: the minimal report or diegetic summary; the partially detailed report, incorporating selected speech utterances; and the fully detailed, maximal report.

In providing a minimal report, the novelist is not concerned with emphasizing any particular feature of a given speech event, but only registers its occurrence. No details are specifically alluded to, nor are instances of reported speech generally incorporated within it. The following examples will suffice.

> Raskolnikov . . . explained his business shortly and
> coherently, in clear and exact terms . . . (240)

"Even later ... when he began giving me answers that
chimed so well with the facts that I was quite surprised,
even then I didn't believe a word he said!" (435)

Raskolnikov repeated his deposition ... (511)

In each instance, the act of reporting certain information is
registered, but with virtually no attendant details forthcoming.

In the partially detailed report, a character's reaction to a
given event is emphasized, or a specific detail of an episode is
highlighted to the virtual exclusion of others; some feature is
stressed, generally by the incorporation of reported speech into
the account.[1] Such emphases may be explicitly documented
through quotation as direct speech; they may be implied (or
veiled) through various devices as indirect speech; or they may
appear as a more complex variation of the two as quasi-direct
speech.[2] To the extent that speech is intended to take account
of speech, the inclusion of certain utterances within dialogue
in general is designed to yield a special emphasis made suitable
and presumably effective to the intention at hand. Thus, when
it is asserted that—

Katerina Ivanovna had gone off "to look for justice"
(390)

—the terrible hopelessness of her entire situation is summed
up in the final two words attributed to the hapless woman
herself.

Although the broad descriptive approach taken here
embraces a whole spectrum of possibility, the several kinds of
reported speech contexts do not lend themselves to neat, com-
partmentalized distinctions. There is the risk of incomplete
description, on the one hand, and overlapping of categories, on
the other. Yet neither concern outweighs the potential for
wide-ranging inclusion of generic possibility within such
descriptive effort. For our purposes, by contrast to its bare

minimal counterpart, the partially detailed account is conceived as bearing a fragment of reported speech in the form of
directly cited discourse, as in the instance just noted, or indirectly cited, as the following will illustrate.

At one point, Raskolnikov briefly recounts to Sonya a
remark he had made earlier to Luzhin.

> "Listen . . . not long ago I told an offensive fellow that
> he was not worth your little finger . . . " (309)

In this instance, the original sense and meaning of the words
are retained. Between the present speaker and the reported
speech there is a clear coinciding or parallelism of both intonation and intention. What Raskolnikov said then he still means
now. (That present speech and reported speech belonging to
the same speaker need not guarantee such parallelism will be
made evident below.)

Similarly, when Sonya reflects upon Raskolnikov's words,
both their meaning and intent are retained, since her surprise
and confusion do not alter or distort the original message.

> "What was that he had said to her? He had kissed her
> foot and said . . . said (yes, he had said it clearly) that
> he could not live without her . . . Oh, heavens." (317)

By contrast, when Raskolnikov admonishes Sonya, he does
not preserve the fervent belief inherent in her words.

> "You must judge things seriously and directly at last,
> and not weep like a child and cry that God won't allow
> it." (316)

Rather, his entirely different (hostile) intonation (regarding
her faith in a benevolent Being) serves to distort their initial
contextual meaning through parodic ridicule.

In sum, in the first instance, when recapitulating his own utterance, Raskolnikov retains its original intent; in the second, Sonya also retains the sense of his words but adds a further (intonational) response of her own ("Oh, heavens!"); in the third, by contrast, he intentionally undermines her meaning. Yet, in all such instances, the incorporation of reported speech (in however small fragment) is bound to isolate and thereby highlight a crystallized piece of information that, as a result, becomes subject to further consideration and interpretation.

In the fully detailed, maximal report, the reader is presented an entire account of events, including the characters' direct speech relevant to that account. In this case, then, the other modes of report may also appear embedded. This implies two linked notions, concisely formulated: first, "Reported speech is embedded speech"; second, "To study embedded speech acts is to study the making—and still more interesting, the breaking—of frames" (Morson 1978:414,415). In this chapter, we will do both. In the interest of brevity, the "frames" themselves will suffice to provide a sense of the expansive communication contained within extended passages, representing in their entirety instances of the maximal report. Hence the following opening and concluding authorial observations.

> Raskolnikov's thoughts were whirling like a tornado. (244)
> . . . .
> All this, like lightning, went racing through his head. (245)

Contained within these frames are a series of confused strategies and suspicions, coupled with an alternating sense of confidence and the lack of it, ranging in extended, painful detail over an entire page.

> Raskolnikov was silent, but watched and listened, still scowling angrily. (322)
>
> ·
>
> Raskolnikov did not answer, but sat pale and motionless, watching Porfiry's face with the same strained attention. (327)

Here within a span of more than four pages, Raskolnikov utters only two words (an affirmative response as to whether he had been studying law), while within the context of these frames is contained the incessant chatter of Porfiry Petrovich, launched as the opening volley of a verbal assault that runs essentially the entire chapter (IV:5).

The maximal account may also serve to document reported inner speech, including the following rumination.

> "'Three ways are open to her,' he thought, 'to throw herself into the canal, to end in a madhouse or . . . or, finally, to abandon herself to debauchery that will numb her mind and turn her heart to stone.'" (310)

While this instance is much briefer than the previous two more extensive cases, a single word or epithet may in fact constitute an entire dialogical response or instance of reported inner speech. Such epithets may also be directed toward various referents during a single meeting. Thus, Raskolnikov's inner expressions of anger, suspicion, and uncertainty are variously directed as follows: "Fool!" (240) refers to the ungainly Razumikhin; "He knows!" (241) is directed toward the wily detective; "Stupid! Weak!" (242) reflects his assessment of his own previous, unguarded utterance; while the more general evaluation, "Ach, how obvious and base!" (255), encompasses the entire awkward situation—a degenerative dialogue, which serves the purposes of one of its participants, while ensnaring the other.

Of related interest are the interconnections among the three forms of report here outlined—their boundaries or the frames separating them. From a temporal perspective, such reports may effect a shift in novelistic time: from present to past (and, ultimately, back to present again as the narrative resumes its principal account). Thus, while each meeting takes place in the present, there are numerous references to the past, including the very recent past, occurring within the time frame of the given meeting itself. As a case in point, when Raskolnikov observes to Sonya—

> "You say Katerina Ivanovna's mind is deranged; your
> own mind is deranged . . . " (308)

—the first statement includes a fragment of reported speech uttered by Sonya directly only moments before; the latter remark, referring to Sonya herself, represents the direct speech of the protagonist articulated in the present. Here past and present utterances nearly coincide in their temporal relation; the past, in other words, is almost immediately (once again) made present.

That recognition affords an insight into the role of reported speech in general. Reported speech is essentially a reconstruction of a past utterance, affording new present significance. Reported speech makes the past once again present by revivifying and vitalizing it with the present significance which prompts its renewed evocation in the first place. This is accomplished by its being incorporated within a new dialogical context, as when Raskolnikov takes Sonya's apt (past) expression and reapplies it in the present.

Concerning distinctions among possible frames, the following passage, in which Raskolnikov informs Sonya that he is aware of the sad origins of her profession, will serve to illustrate the transitional nature of the three forms of report just outlined.

> "Your father told me about it, that time. He told me all
> about you . . . About how you went out at six o'clock
> and came back after eight, and about how Katerina
> Ivanovna knelt by your bed." (304)

If not further detailed by what follows, the first two statements
would constitute a minimal report affirming only the fact that
a talk had taken place. However, in subsequent elaboration
(post ellipses), oblique reference is made to specific poignant
details, which tolerate no further explicit mention. Yet a subtle
transition has nevertheless been effected—from an initial, minimal form of report to the partial type (incorporating Mar-
meladov's words as indirect reported speech), which, in turn,
does emphasize certain sad telling detail.

In recounting her relationship with Katerina Ivanovna,
Sonya recalls an instance of the latter's making an uncharac-
teristic, fanciful request:

> "'Make me a present of them, Sonya, please,' she said.
> She said *please*, and she so wanted them." (306)

She also regrets her own unthinking refusal:

> "What use are they to you, Katerina Ivanovna?" I said.
> Yes, that is how I spoke to her, "what use". (307)

In contrast to the previous instance, in this artificially seg-
mented passage the transition is twice effected from the maximal form of report, where the entire utterance—however brief—is
presented, to the partially detailed form, where the emphasis
falls upon the single word or phrase ("please"; "what use"),
which, upon recollection, triggers a feeling of anguish. The two
reports are seen to alternate, as the maximal form takes initial
precedence to provide a complete account through the inclusion of direct speech. However, it immediately yields to the
partially detailed form, which points up the exceptional poig-

nancy of the moment, recalled by emphasizing the single most crucial utterance at each stage of a very small but memorable drama.

On occasion, the frames between the various forms of report are difficult to discern, since reported speech itself may exist on the boundaries of dialogue (as quasi-direct discourse). As a case in point, Sonya confesses her grief in a moment of sadness:

> "But I am ... dishonored ... I am a great, great sinner."

And Raskolnikov, in turn, responds:

> "I said it not because of your dishonor and your sin,
> but because of your great suffering." (309)

The phrase "dishonor and sin" clearly refers to Sonya's preceding remark, although these are not precisely her words. At the same time they do not belong to Raskolnikov either, since their point of origin must be traced to Sonya's utterance. Within the present context, then, they exist on the borders of dialogic speech, exemplifying, in effect, Bakhtin's observation that "Discourse lives, as it were, on the boundary between its own context and another, alien, context" (1981:284), where "alien" (however sinister sounding) refers, simply, to another person's speech. Raskolnikov's utterance is thus situated on the border of his own intention and meaning, and Sonya's. Yet within this context, one can state with assurance only that the words, while uttered by Raskolnikov as variants of Sonya's, are clearly engaged in dialogical interaction, the one speech utterance with another.

A moment later Raskolnikov observes: "That you are a great sinner is true." Here the words "great sinner" indisputably belong to Sonya, but significantly, are employed with a different intonation and in a different sense—that is, dialogically, by Raskolnikov, who concludes that she has sinned primarily against herself ("but your greatest sin is that you have destroyed

and betrayed yourself *in vain*" 309). In accord with the dialogical nature of the novel in general (as Bakhtin would have it) and
of the present work in particular, the view expressed by Raskolnikov with regard to Sonya is one she will subsequently take of
him upon learning of his crime: "What have you done, what
have you done to yourself?" (394). Furthermore, it will resonate
one last time in Raskolnikov's own view of himself, as he confesses to her: "I killed myself, not that old woman!" (402). In
registering such "resonance," a claim for the contrapuntal nature of the novel's dialogically engaged discourse rings especially true.

In brief summation, our aim is to demonstrate that in ana-
lyzing dialogic structures, the dimension and scope of the information provided may be regarded in terms of whether it is
conveyed only minimally, is partially detailed, or affords a fully
detailed account (allowing in the latter two modes for the
incorporation of reported speech as added significant detail).
Moreover, the frames between and connecting such reports are
themselves significant in terms of dialogic relations, and need
to be further explored as such. Last, our intent is explicitly to
sketch at least the lineaments of a broadly descriptive model,
within whose framework might be suitably contained the mani-
festly complex dialogic structures inherent in verbal art.

To this end, the possibly varying intentions between the
reported speech and the reporting context (the speaker or
author) must be distinguished as a means of determining the
degree of parallelism or coincidence between the aims of the
one and the other. On the one hand, the reporting context may
utilize the utterances construed as reported in a manner not
coincident with original intentions, as suggested by Voloshinov:
"The impetus for weakening the peripheries of the utterance
may originate in the author's context, in which case that context permeates the reported speech with its own intonation . . . "
(Porfiry's account of Raskolnikov's theory, as will be shown,
illustrates the point.) On the other hand, the converse may also

be true, when reported speech dominates the reporting context: "The verbal dominant may shift to the reported speech, which in that case becomes more forceful and more active than the authorial context framing it. This time the reported speech begins to resolve, as it were, the reporting context . . . " (1973: 121). (Raskolnikov's report of his own idea will be shown paradoxically to illustrate the case.) The question ever pertinent to dialogue, then, is not simply *whose* words are being uttered at a given moment, but *how* are they employed. Whose intentions, in other words, are being fulfilled?

This problem will find its place in the ensuing discussion, where the dual purpose is to analyze (from a different perspective than previously) the several alternating meetings between student and detective, and murderer and prostitute, as dialogic structures contained by the framework just outlined. Further, the applicability and effectiveness of such a model will be implicitly demonstrated in the process. As Voloshinov declares in programmatic fashion, "the true object of inquiry ought to be precisely the dynamic interrelationship of . . . the speech being reported (the other person's speech) and the speech doing the reporting (the author's speech)" (1973:119). To realize this aim through concrete analysis constitutes the present effort.

*

Reported speech may be regarded as embedded discourse or as discourse belonging to one speaker grafted onto that of another. Subsequent discussion will serve to support this understanding. However, to regard an utterance as being "embedded" within or "grafted" upon another is to apply figurative usage to a concrete endeavor—that of isolating or separating one speech fragment from its larger context. Moreover, that very effort (again expressed figuratively) may itself be likened to distinguishing precisely where one dark hue in a Rembrandt painting ends and another begins. Yet neither consideration need preclude assailing the job all the same. So, as an example of embedded discourse, let us consider the following passage, which precedes Sonya's reading of the raising of Lazarus, a striking instance of a subtext employed to evoke a climactic moment in the novel.

> Raskolnikov half understood why Sonya could not make herself read to him, and the more he understood, the more roughly and irritably he persisted. He knew very well how difficult it was for her to expose and betray all that was *her own*. He understood that those feelings in fact constituted her real long-standing *secret*, cherished perhaps since her girlhood, in the midst of her family, with an unhappy father, a stepmother crazed by grief, and hungry children, in an atmosphere of hideous shrieks and reproaches. At the same time he now knew and knew for certain that although she was troubled and feared something terrible if she were to read now, yet she had a tormenting desire to read, and read for *him* to hear, and read *now*, "whatever might happen afterwards" . . . He could see all this in her eyes and in her emotional agitation . . .
> (313)

The first sentence of the passage, with its distanced objectivity, belongs to the author. The second, however, already serves as a kind of linkage, leading from that sense of objectivity to the necessarily subjective interiority of the main character, underscored by the italicicized expression "her own," representing Raskolnikov's perception of her. Moreover, each italicized expression embedded within the narrative represents no longer the author's but Raskolnikov's own unsettling (for Sonya), perspicacious insight. The last sentence of the passage again frames Raskolnikov's transmuted thoughts. Only at its close are we once again in the realm of the author's word exclusively, which distances the reader from the interiority of his character and, at the same time, from that character's entirely credible apperception and assessment of another character.

Earlier, Raskolnikov had strenuously and perversely attempted to strip the child harlot of her sustaining illusion.

"And what will become of you?"
. . . .
"Well, but what will happen now?" (305)
. . . .
"And the children? Where can they go then, except here?"
. . . .
"Well, if you become ill and are taken to hospital . . . what will happen then?"
. . . .
"Cannot happen? . . . Are you insured against it? Then what will become of them?" (307)
. . . .
"You don't get money every day?"
. . . .
"Perhaps God does not even exist . . . " (308)
. . . .
" . . . you are helping nobody . . . and not saving anybody from anything . . . " (309)
. . . .
"And what does God do for you . . . ?" (311)

Having ravaged her in this inquisitorial manner, perhaps no less than others, it is he who now perceives her bared, as it were, and yet still obliges the girl to make that further revelation of what is *her own* and of the spirit. Thus, on the one hand, Raskolnikov is able to take note of the fact that she remains morally unscathed by the depravity upon which her life and, more importantly for her, the lives of her family, depend. ("All her shame had obviously touched her only mechanically; no trace of real corruption had yet crept into her heart; he could see that; it was her real self that stood before him . . . " 310).

Yet, at the same time, because of his own suffering and resultant insensitivity, coupled with the terrible need to penetrate
to the core of her being (prior to throwing himself at her feet),
he is incapable of seeing that he, too, attempts in invidious
fashion to touch the girl and reduce her to the shameful state
of being at once visible ("it was her real self that stood before
him") and immediately *perceptible*. And he both succeeds and
fails: succeeds in finding the purity he has sought in her; fails
in rending her protective cloak, as do all the others, we may
assume, who come to her with cash. For Sonya is protected, an
untouchable, whose moral purity remains intact as *her own*—
and as Raskolnikov correctly perceives: since it is his key words
filtered through and embedded within the previously cited
authorial discourse that are most expressly revealing of the
girl's special character and evangelical motivation.

During the course of her reading, the power of the story—in
simplest form—finds its fullest dramatization in Dostoevsky's
art. Sonya, as Raskolnikov comes to understand, is protected by
story, myth, fable, or parable; whatever it might be for others,
for her it is the Word, the unadulterated truth, and it both
cloaks and shields her from the horror of the lie, which, as she
understands it, is constituted by mundane reality alone and her
ephemeral existence within it. Thus Raskolnikov clearly perceives her *secret*, and that she is reading for *him* to hear, and is
reading *now*, "whatever might happen afterwards," as a kind of
willingly fulfilled obligation imposed upon her by her faith.

In contrast to the previously cited passage, where fine distinctions are made among seemingly undifferentiated "hues,"
in the following description of Sonya's animated features, we
clearly distinguish the referential speech of the author from his
character's strangely exultant but silent exclamation concluding the passage.

> He looked with a new, strange, almost painful feeling
> at that thin, pale, angular little face, at those timid blue

eyes that were capable of flashing with such fire, such stern, strong feeling, at that small figure, still shaking with indignation and anger, and it all seemed to him more and more strange, almost impossible. "Yurodivaya! yurodivaya!" he repeated firmly to himself. (311)

Here only the repeated epithet, conventionally set off by quotation marks as the character's innermost thought—in this instance, a sudden realization appearing as a kind of epiphany—may be seen as clearly separate from the extended observation preceding it. In effect, such instance of reported (inner) speech is attributed to one character but clearly specifies another—in the sense of being an identifying sign of that other ("Yurodivaya! yurodivaya!"), as one beyond the lure of worldly affairs and their inevitable taint.

Finally, as a striking instance of speech being "grafted" onto speech (as quasi-direct discourse), we read what appears to be straightforward authorial comment. "She looked at him without understanding. She knew only that he was terribly and infinitely unhappy" (316). However, as a consequence of Raskolnikov's relentless probing of Sonya's "almost *insatiable* compassion," it becomes evident that the concluding, sympathetic phrase cannot be attributed to the author. Rather, it belongs to another voice entirely—that of the frail girl pitilessly interrogated by her late-night visitor, while herself remaining securely oblivious to all verbal assault by virtue of being protected by the omnipresent Word. After her interlocutor has finally made his departure, the reader is provided in the form of direct speech with her subsequent thoughts, including the following rumination: "Oh, he must be *terribly unhappy!*" (317; italics added). While the words are identical to those seemingly belonging to authorial observation, they are indisputably hers—in both cases.

The idea that previous utterances almost inevitably play a significant role in ensuing dialogue is continually affirmed by

Bakhtin. "The word is born in a dialogue as a living rejoinder within it; the word is shaped in dialogic interaction with an alien word that is already in the object" (1981:279). This view is confirmed within extended dialogue during the first meeting between Raskolnikov and Porfiry Petrovich, where the previous day's heated conversation, devoted to the question of whether crime exists ("is there or is there not such a thing as crime?" 245), emerges as the ostensible subject of their discussion.

At the start, the current socialist position is summed up by Razumikhin in thoroughly negative, unsympathetic fashion.

> "Nature is not taken into account.... it all comes down to the question of comfort. A very easy solution of the problem! It is so clear-cut, and there is no need to think! That is the main point—you needn't think. The whole mystery of life can be put on two sheets of printed paper!" (245-46)

In this case, the semantic weight of the statement clearly falls upon the speaker's reaction to his subject rather than upon its substance, which is immediately subordinated to a negative evaluation. More important, the pattern is almost immediately repeated in subtler terms during Porfiry's only thinly veiled, similarly unsympathetic account of Raskolnikov's "idea."

That Porfiry is consistently in control throughout the discussion is evident. He is not taken in by his visitors' "uncontrolled" entrance, orchestrated by Raskolnikov, nor does he take special cognizance of their frowning countenances upon their departure. At one point, he leaves the room, returns a moment later, taking a different tack ("he began in a quite different tone, smiling"), and quickly directs the conversation toward the subject of crime, intentionally provoking Razumikhin's fully expected, incensed account of their discussion the day before. ("He was growing visibly more animated, and he kept laughing as he looked at Razumikhin . . . " 245).

Since Raskolnikov had not appeared on the previous day, as expected, Porfiry simply restages what had taken place then—orchestrating, in turn, his own theater for the ostensible benefit of his hilarity-prone visitor. Having allowed Razumikhin the opportunity to express his disenchantment with the socialist view of crime, the detective recalls with studied casualness Raskolnikov's article on crime ("Apropos of all these questions . . . I have just remembered . . . an article of yours . . . " 247). His disingenuous "recollection" affords Porfiry the opportunity to air seemingly inadvertently his own disenchantment. In doing so, he obliges the article's properly astonished author to recapitulate its contents—a task in which the detective purposefully assists. But first, the clever strategist summarizes the one central idea himself.

> "In a word, you introduce, if you remember, a hint to the effect that there are persons who are able . . . or rather, not who are able but who have every right, to commit any wrong or crime, and that laws, so to say, are not made for them."
>
> . . . .
>
> "The point is that in his article people are somehow divided into two classes, the 'ordinary' and the 'extraordinary.' The ordinary ones must live in submission and have no right to transgress the laws, because, you see, they are ordinary. And the extraordinary have the right to commit any crime and break every kind of law just because they are extraordinary." (248)

Thus is Raskolnikov's idea initially presented in summary fashion by an unsympathetic, alien voice. Clearly, Porfiry's feigned efforts at delicacy ("if you remember"), his hesitancy (. . .), and concomitant searching for the proper manner of expression ("or rather, not who are able but who have every right") do not conceal his distaste for the whole notion ("break every kind of law"). Nor are these conscious devices meant to

do so. Rather, they are intended to be transparent and provocative. And they accomplish their ends, as Raskolnikov's own
reaction confirms ("Raskolnikov smiled at this forced and
deliberate perversion of his idea" 248). Moreover, as a kind of
"arena in which *two* intonations, *two* points of view, *two* speech
acts converge and clash" (Voloshinov 1973:135), Porfiry's account incorporates—in far subtler fashion than Razumikhin
previously expressed himself—a separate embedded message
expressing his own reaction to what he himself is communicating. In effect, Porfiry's strategy exemplifies what Voloshinov
terms the "linguistic essence of indirect discourse," defined by
him as "That essence [which] consists in the analytical transmission of someone's speech. An analysis simultaneous with
and inseparable from transmission constitutes the obligatory
hallmark of all modifications of indirect discourse whatever"
(1973:128). Such analysis is here neatly exemplified by Porfiry's simultaneous summation *and* negative assessment of
Raskolnikov's theory.

The key notion of that theory—that the bearer of a "new
word" may *eliminate* "obstacles" in his path to greatness—has
a bearing both upon the past, in Raskolnikov's own "over-
stepping" of societal bounds, and the future, in the intensified
continuation of the cat and mouse game that has just been
initiated. Porfiry's efforts, in this and subsequent meetings,
are directed at driving Raskolnikov's impassioned rhetoric—
whether ostensibly expressed in print or orally—to its logical
conclusion. Accordingly, he conveys the terrible implica-tions
of Raskolnikov's theory by intentionally transmitting the message itself in a banal manner designed to make it appear woe-
fully unprepossessing. His stark formulation of the idea thus
reduces it, in bare terms (which are his own), to a dreary set of
precepts: "people are divided into two classes; The ordinary...
have no right . . . because . . . they are ordinary; And the
extraordinary have the right . . . because they are extraordinary." Furthermore, in such bland, matter-of-fact tones he

underscores the element of horror and lawlessness by blatantly juxtaposing "form and content" (the idea with its delivery) in calculated, discordant fashion. To this end, he employs an uncertain but colloquial manner of expression, deliberately contrasted to the anti-social notion itself (permitting the "extraordinary ones" to commit "any crime"), which makes it all the more abhorrent to its listeners. "Thus almost every word in the narrative (as concerns its expressivity, its emotional coloring, its accentual position in the phrase) figures simultaneously in two intersecting contexts, two speech acts: in the speech of the author-narrator (ironic and mocking) and the speech of the hero (who is far removed from this irony)" (Voloshinov 1973:136). In such abstract theoretical terms is the present dialogue fully encompassed. Moreover, in thematic terms, the author-narrator-detective's clever linguistic stratagem proves successful, as an agitated Razumikhin stammers in response: "How can it be? He can't possibly have said that!" (248). While Raskolnikov himself, at whom it has all been directed, decides "to accept the challenge" (249).

Having been put in such defensive position, it is left to Raskolnikov to rebutt this usurped, initial presentation of his theory. In undertaking the task, he presents his own synopsis of the article, representing the centerpiece of the entire dialogue, in relatively balanced, judicious manner ("he began simply and modestly" 249) in what has here been termed a maximal report. He ends his response on a challenging note of its own ("until we have built the New Jerusalem" 251), which contrasts not only with Porfiry's deliberately provocative account but, more importantly, with Raskolnikov's own later, deprecating recapitulation.

He begins by ironically acknowledging Porfiry's "accurate" assessment, but then goes on to declare that he had not insisted that extraordinary individuals are necessarily obliged to commit crimes, as Porfiry, according to Raskolnikov, had presumably stated. ("I do not in the least insist that the extraordinary people are absolutely bound and obliged to commit offences on any and every occasion, as you say I do.") Oddly, Porfiry had not made the point, nor had he specifically attributed it to the former student. Hence the reader receives a certain "fabricated" reported speech that will not prove unique in the subsequent course of their talks. However, Raskolnikov does affirm that if genius is hindered in its strivings, it becomes incumbent for it to "overstep" whatever "obstacles" might stand in the way. On the one hand, he observes, no one has the right wantonly to commit crime ("go out stealing from market-stalls every day" 249), on the other, he firmly takes his stand with the leaders and "blood-letters" (*krovoprolivcy*) by affirming his view thus:

> "In a word, I deduce that all of them, not only the great ones, but also those who diverge ever so slightly from the beaten track, those, that is, who are just barely capable of saying something just a little bit new, must, by their nature, inevitably be criminals— in a greater or less degree, naturally." (249-250)

Here his repeated use of qualifications ("not only the great ones"; "ever so slightly"; "just barely capable"; "in greater or less degree") and telling diminutive ("just a little bit new" [*čto-to noven'koe* VI,200]) indicate Raskolnikov's willingness to allow a certain breadth to his elitist category, which thus affords a place for those who might make only a small contribution towards altering the lot of mankind. The former student's paradoxical aspiration to find himself in such mongrel company (those who diverge/criminals) does not escape notice by the astute detective, who has succeeded in putting him on the defensive regarding his guiding principle. ("In short, you see that up to this point there is nothing specially new here.") And rightly so, for the question may be fairly posed—in what can Raskolnikov's own "new word" be said to consist? Especially when he himself acknowledges that his division of the world into cannon fodder and generals is nothing new. Beyond this he must have an idea of his own, some governing notion that affords him "the right to overstep" ("to march over corpses, or wade through blood" 250) and which would place him squarely in the category of those who are to "move the world and guide it to its goal" (251). This he lacks, having failed to distinguish an essentially static notion, which categorizes, defines, and tells how it is in the world, from one which is dynamic, motivational, and therefore, changes the world. Amounting to an old and hardly original taxonomy vulgarly expressed as—"there are two kinds of people in the world"—Raskolnikov's idea (" . . . people being, by the law of nature, divided *in general* into two categories . . . " 250) is thus not synonymous with that kind which distinguishes genius from the masses, while offering the latter new insights and more advanced goals.

His entire thought fails, then, on two counts. First, as he himself perceives, it is superfluous from the start. For if one wonders if one is a Napoleon, one is decidedly not. Such crucial realization comes slowly however, and—as a turning point in the novel, leading to Raskolnikov's eventual submission—only after the crime is committed. Second, by not being dynamic but only taxonomic, his idea does not afford him any "rights" whatever, according to his own stated criteria. Thus the question arises—for what reason need he have killed in the first place, if there were no subsequent plan to justify his having "overstepped"? This is a question which Raskolnikov does not ask (in dialogue with Sonya). Moreover, it is one which Porfiry, who poses a host of attendant related questions, cannot logically ask (since it would have to be predicated upon the firm knowledge that Raskolnikov had indeed perpetrated the crime). But it is precisely the one which Sonya does ask—and which Raskolnikov can neither satisfactorily (from his own perspective) nor convincingly (from hers) answer. Hence, these two linked considerations indicate paradoxically that Raskolnikov's idea is not an idea by his own definition. It is not the kind, in other words, which affords the right to overstep. Not only do the original premises not hold but they are themselves both an indication and a source of the inherent inconsistencies which finally invalidate the idea for its author himself.

At this stage, however, of the hero's disenchantment with his former guiding principle, Porfiry's initial transmission of the idea, coupled with the author's subsequent expansion of the topic, allows the detective to raise certain disconcerting problems: Could not some confusion arise in attempting to distinguish members of one group from the other? Suppose "some young man" finds himself in straitened circumstances just prior to launching his future campaign (and must find a way to obtain the needed funds)? Might not even Raskolnikov have considered himself a possible member of such an elite group? But the final, crushing blow is effected from an unexpected quarter, when from a corner of the room the hitherto silent Zametov suddenly exclaims: "Wasn't it indeed some future Napoleon who last week dispatched our Alena Ivanovna with an axe?" (255).

The answer to that disturbing question is formulated repeatedly by Raskolnikov himself at his second meeting with Sonya, during which he intends to tell her who killed her friend Lizaveta. In fact, as noted, he never does *tell* her. She is obliged to read the terrible truth in his pained, contorted features. Yet he does attempt to explain why he had committed the murder— in a manner that alternately confuses and astounds his child-like interlocutor ("A human being a louse!" 399). That same manner, however, also reflects his own confusion and growing disillusionment with his previously motivating idea. His disenchantment is made especially evident upon his second recounting of his ill-considered theory. For on this occasion, what he conveys to an uncomprehending "innocent" incapable of comprehending ("Who made me a judge of who shall live and

who shall not?" 391) conforms more closely with Porfiry's deprecating, cursory account than with his own initial exposition.
While that telling had been relatively direct and straight-for-
ward, suggesting some measure of retained self-assurance, his
account to Sonya is related ironically, revealing a lack of conviction and even discomfiture with a notion that he had only
recently gamely defended.

> "This was it: I wanted to make myself a Napoleon, and
> that is why I killed her . . . Now do you understand?"
> (397)

Thus, in strange, ironic reversal, knowing full well that he is
dissimulating rather than communicating, he challenges Sonya
to understand—just as previously he had been challenged to
make the thing lucid to those who could understand all too well.
And, just as he had been destined to fail on that occasion—because, paradoxically, it was already eminently clear to his
perspicacious interlocutor of the time just what it all amounted
to—here he will not succeed with a girl who could never understand.

> "The point is this: on one occasion, I put this question
> to myself: what if, for example, Napoleon had found
> himself in my shoes, with no Toulon, no Egypt, no
> crossing of Mont Blanc, to give his career a start, but,
> instead of those monumental and glorious things, with
> simply one ridiculous old woman, who must be killed
> to get money from her trunk (for that career of his, you
> understand?)—well, would he have made up his mind
> to do it if there was no other way? Would he have shrunk
> from it, because it was so un-monumental and . . . and
> so sinful? Well, I tell you I tormented myself over that
> 'problem' for a terribly long time, and I was terribly
> ashamed when at last I realized (suddenly somehow)
> that not only would he not shrink, but the idea would
> never even enter his head that it was not monu-

> mental . . . and he would be quite unable to understand
> what there was to shrink from. And if there had been
> no other way open to him, he would have strangled her,
> without giving her a chance to speak, and without a
> moment's hesitation! . . . Well, I also . . . stopped
> hesitating . . . strangled her . . . following the example
> of my authority . . . And that is exactly how it was!
> Does that amuse you? Yes, Sonya, perhaps the most
> amusing thing about all this, is that that is exactly how
> it happened . . . " (397-98)

Such, for the most part (excluding the "frames"), represents Raskolnikov's reported *inner* speech. What is striking here is that Raskolnikov serves as both the reporting context (as speaker) and the source of the reported speech (as author)—and yet the two intentions do not coincide. The original idea had run aground of its psychological consequences. Thus, in effect, its author carries forward in unwitting but devastating fashion the work initiated by the detective.

The tone of his account from the start is mocking and derisive ("what if, for example, Napoleon had found himself in my shoes . . . ?"). The manner of expression is ironic ("instead of those monumental and glorious things"; "simply one ridiculous old woman") or seemingly odd and disjointed ("so un-monumental and . . . "); it is peculiarly off-handed ("for that career of his, you understand?") and inappropriately casual ("Well, I tell you . . . ")—all of which features reflect an intonational conflict between a potentially direct, straightforward manner of expression as opposed to an (actually employed) indirect, ironic form, which clashes with the real gravity of the subject. In addition, the consistent infelicitous choice of expression is further augmented by a sustained sense of hesitancy ("and . . . and so sinful"), awkwardness ("following the example of my authority"), and uncertainty ("suddenly somehow"), the combined effect of which leads to an extended, inconclusive final note riddled with ellipses and punctuated by a heightened fear of further ridicule ("Does that amuse you?"), which Raskolnikov himself appears to invite ("perhaps the most amusing thing about all this, is . . . "). Finally, the entire statement is steeped in an adolescent indulgence in casuistry ("at last I realized . . . that the idea would never even enter his head"), which, as the hapless student himself recognizes, heralds—by his own logic—the gaping flaw in his thinking. In semiotic terms, the entire speech may be viewed as a signifier, whose signified consists in the message's own fated capitulation to another, superseding idea: that the original had miscarried.

How this superseding idea achieves its prominence may be detailed in part through brief consideration of Raskolnikov's "confession" to Sonya from the perspective of the series of explanations he offers for having committed the crime.

(1) "It was to rob her!" (395)

(2) "I wanted to make myself a Napoleon . . . " (397)

(3) "I was their only hope . . . . I could not keep myself at the university and was obliged to leave it for a time . . . . Meanwhile, my mother would have withered away with care and grief . . . .and so I decided, having got hold of the old woman's money . . . to make a completely new career for myself . . . " (398-99)

(4) "I only killed a louse . . . a useless, vile, pernicious louse." (399)

(5) "I realized . . . that power is given only to the man who dares swoop and take it. There is only one thing needed, only one—to dare! . . . I wanted to have the courage, and I killed . . . I only wanted to dare . . . that was the only reason!" (400-401)

In fact, none of these constitutes the "whole reason." Moreover, these rationales cancel out one another (or diminish their respective credibility) by virtue, simply, of their extensive proliferation. Raskolnikov himself reduces the stature of his own argument, in other words, each time he offers a new explanation as a substitute for a previous one (none of which qualifies in any case to be regarded as visionary in the first place). In addition, he provides a counterargument or explicit negation of each in turn, as the following statements correlated with those preceding clearly indicate.

(1) "I don't know . . . I had not decided whether I should take the money or not. " (396)
      "And, most important, it was not money that I needed . . . when I killed; it was not money so much as something else . . . " (402)

(2) "If I worried for so long about whether Napoleon would have done it or not, it must be because I felt clearly that I was not Napoleon . . . " (401)

(3) "I told you just now that I couldn't keep myself at the university. But do you know, I might perhaps have done it?" (399)
      "I did not commit murder to help my mother—that's rubbish! I did not commit murder in order to use the profit and power I gained to make myself a benefactor to humanity. Rubbish!" (401-402)

(4) "Of course I know she wasn't a louse . . . " (399)
      "You don't think that I didn't know . . . . that, if I asked myself, 'Is a man a louse?' it meant that *for me* he was not, although he might be one for a man to whom the question never even occurred, and who would march straight ahead without asking any questions at all?" (401)

(5) "You don't think, either, that I didn't know . . . that if I began questioning and cross-examining myself about whether I had the right to take power, that meant that I hadn't any such right?" (401)

Finally, he offers one last explanation: "What I needed to find out then . . . was whether I was capable of stepping over the barriers or not . . . . Listen: when I went to the old woman's that time, it was only *to test myself* . . . "—to which he immediately offers the conclusive deconstructive correlative, by exclaiming: "I killed myself, not that old woman! There and then I murdered myself at one blow, for ever!" (402). This, then, is his answer. Having equated man in the abstract with a louse, and having striven in grotesque manner to rise above the lowly status he had thus designated, he finds he has not achieved his end—and eventually discovers his own humanity in the process. But this is something which, like a birth, occurs gradually and painfully, and is only hinted at towards the close of the novel, whose overall purpose is to document instead the self-ordained trial leading to that potential self-discovery.

In sum, Raskolnikov's idea is presented, first of all, to Porfiry, who proceeds to conduct a critical analysis of what he has managed to coerce from his young interlocutor. However, when Raskolnikov confesses to Sonya and tries to explain his motive, it is he who conducts his own critical review of what had been his guiding principle, and he himself finds both the idea and its author lacking by his own established criteria. Hence his theory now appears fragmented and in sad disarray. ("No . . . that's all wrong . . . That's not it! . . . No, that's not it; I am getting it wrong again!" 399-400). In essence, his entire discordant account of the rationale behind his ultimately self-assertive act is presented in the form of reported inner speech, in an effort to recount the train of thought which had generated the deed. The series of explanations as to why the murder was committed are themselves past-oriented structures. However, as previously remarked, reported speech is essentially a reconstruction of a past utterance, affording new present significance. As a result, those statements that negate or reduce Raskolnikov's resurrected but unconvincing rationales appear *immediate*, and are therefore substantially more conclusive ("I know all this now ... " 402), since they are initially articulated in the present and are contemporaneous with the narrative itself—with the events of the novel that are currently unfolding in the far more decisive here and now. Having been devalued this time by its author, the idea is no longer viable. Raskolnikov must now own up: he has no idea—and never did. What had appeared to be an idea is reduced to a mere shadow of one, a haunting specter and nothing more.

The dialogue in the second meeting between Raskolnikov and Porfiry may be described as principally the interlarding of what amounts to extended monologue on the part of the detective eager to expound his method. "The business [of an examining magistrate] is . . . a sort of art, in its own way" (324). That "art," as Porfiry elaborates at some length, is designed to snare—in seemingly effortless fashion—the criminal at bay. "If I don't arrest him or worry him . . . but if he knows, or at least suspects . . . that I know everything down to the last detail . . . He will come to me of his own accord . . . " (326). His extended discourse is "countered" only by brief snatches of gloomily defensive interior monologue on the part of Raskolnikov.

> "Why, can he really be trying to distract my attention with this stupid talk?" (323)

> "But why, though, why give me such strong hints? . . . Is he counting on the bad state of my nerves? . . . " (327)

Eventually, his defensiveness inevitably surfaces.

> "But I will not permit anyone to laugh in my face and torment me . . . "
> . . . .
> "I will not permit it . . . Do you hear that . . . I will not permit it!

. . . .
"I will not permit it!" (329)

. . . .
"I won't permit it, I won't permit it!" (330)

In the process, the two forms of discourse (Raskolnikov's interior monologue and overt dialogical response) are intermeshed in sadly contradictory fashion, as he ruminates on possible strategies (his own and the detective's), while simultaneously defeating those in his best interest and being defeated in turn.

> "Can it be possible," flashed through his mind, "that he is lying even now? No, impossible, impossible!" He pushed the thought away from him, realizing in time to what degree of rage and fury it might drive him . . . (332)

Yet that realization does not deter him, but results in a verbal torrent, not long in coming, that only increases in intensity and insulting familiarity as the dialogue continues to deteriorate.

> "You keep on lying . . . " (332)
>
> . . . .
> "You are lying all the time!" (333)
>
> . . . .
> "You are lying all the time! . . . I don't know what you are aiming at, but you do nothing but lie . . . .You are lying!" (334)
>
> . . . .
> "I will not allow myself to be tortured!" (335)
>
> . . . .
> "You are still lying! . . . You lie, you damned clown!" (336)

Finally, the cat has the mouse cornered, seizes him in his jaws, and for the moment delights in containing him there, causing Raskolnikov mournfully to declare:

> "I understand it all, all of it! You are lying. You are teasing me to make me betray myself . . . "

To which Porfiry immediately responds:

> "But you can't betray yourself any further . . . old chap." (336)

Within the context of their seemingly one-sided verbal duel, an added dynamic is introduced by the wily detective, who repeatedly attributes to Raskolnikov utterances never articulated by him. A new opposition is thus instituted between the reporting context and reported speech, where the latter (Raskolnikov's supposed utterances)—through the clever machinations of the former (Porfiry)—is transformed into what amounts to incorporated fictions, intended to lend support to the detective's shrewdly devised, psychologically undermining strategy. In other words, as opposed to "genuine" reported speech that is actually articulated, utterances that have never been stated are nevertheless (falsely) registered. Thus, Porfiry contends that Raskolnikov had made "a very just and penetrating remark" (but the reader is informed: "Raskolnikov had made no such remark" 323); that as a defensive action, he had taken recourse in laughter (but: "Raskolnikov had no idea of laughing . . ." 325); and that he had insisted as a kind of "confession" that he had persuaded Razumikhin to make a special visit to the detective (but again: "Raskolnikov had never done so" 267). In each instance, then, the assertion is inaccurate—but, as part of the detective's overall plan, intentionally so.

As a final, telling instance of Porfiry's strategic insistence upon "false reportage," he twice misquotes Raskolnikov's ill-considered observation that the detective's overall ploy consists precisely in trying to distract him with senseless chatter, "lull his mistrust, and then suddenly and unexpectedly stun him by hitting him on the crown of his head with the most dangerous and fatal question" (321). However, the student's formulation of the detective's plan is reformulated, in turn, by Porfiry, who fully counts on Raskolnikov's further discomfiture.

> "Who is there, tell me, out of all the people accused of crimes, even if they are absolute yokels, who does not know that they will try to lull his mistrust (as you happily express it) with irrelevant questions, and then unexpectedly stun him by hitting him on the crown of his head, *to use your delightful metaphor*, as if with an axe . . . " (324; italics added)

Later, lest the point not be taken, he reiterates, using Raskolnikov's expression again in distorted (misquoted) form to explain his own strategy—the explanation of which constitutes a considerable part of that strategy. The clever detective thus (mis)uses the words of his interlocutor, or simply invents them, to suit his own aim.

> "I gave you that precious detail . . . with both hands, I, an examining magistrate! Don't you see anything in that? If I suspected you at all, should I have done that? On the contrary, I should first have lulled your suspicions, and pretended that I had not been informed of the fact; I should have drawn your attention in the opposite direction, and then stunned you, as with a blow on the head with an axe *(to use your own expression)* . . . " (333; italics added)

In neither instance is the figurative expression pointedly attributed to Raskolnikov really his. Nevertheless, Porfiry's own favored addition to their discussion, his repeated evocation of a "metaphorical" axe, could not have failed to "stun" his quarry.

   In the end, Porfiry goes to Raskolnikov for one last talk "to clear things up," while the latter goes to Sonya prior to beginning his new ordeal. Yet all of their respective dialogues are interconnected in terms of parallelism or contrast, since the focus of their discussions is always the same. At the first meeting between Raskolnikov and Sonya, he serves, in effect, as an inquisitor, demanding to understand the evident contradiction in her life. Similarly, Porfiry serves in a like role during their first meeting. Later, at their second and third, Porfiry essentially monopolizes the talk; Raskolnikov does the same during the latter two meetings with Sonya, who, in a reversal of roles, now serves as his interlocutor, in trying to understand *why*. At the second meeting between Sonya and Raskolnikov, she learns that he is the murderer—a fact which Porfiry already knows and reveals in the course of their subsequent, final talk. The crucial information emanating from Raskolnikov, which is at the center of all their respective dialogues, thus comes full circle back to him; what he does not so much *tell* as intimate to Sonya, who intuits the fact from what she *sees*, he is later told, in turn, by Porfiry. Yet both the girl and the detective—she at their second, he at their final encounter—advise him of the same thing: that in order to live, he must expiate his crime.

At their third meeting, Porfiry reconstructs for his astounded listener virtually every occurrence that had served as both the source of his earlier suspicions and the basis for his current conviction. Thus, among a whole series of astute observations, he remarks: "And when we began to examine your article, and you expounded your meaning—every one of your words could be taken in two senses, as if there were another word hidden beneath it!" (434). That notion, extended to include every instance of reported speech as potentially bearing (at least) two interlarded meanings or intentions, is emblematic of our present concern. In effect, Porfiry's statement—contextually bound in verbal art—serves to confirm Voloshinov's previously noted abstract theoretical point: that, in the transmission of another's speech, there is an attendant analysis accomplished simultaneously with that transmission; the present speaker or "reporting context," in other words, leaves *his* imprint upon the speech reported. This is the case, as we have seen, even when that context and the source of that (reported) speech are identical, in which case (Raskolnikov's account to Sonya of his theory), the underlying intentions may still differ.

Throughout the detective's entire lengthy discourse, again Raskolnikov hardly articulates a word, until he finally manages to stammer—

"Then . . . who . . . committed the murder?" (437)

—and learns that he was right from the start: Porfiry *knows*: *he* is the murderer. His immediate reaction is to deny what they both know to be true. But now the cat will not let his prey out of his grasp quite so easily. Raskolnikov must own up, and to this end, Porfiry allows him a small grace period—enough time, in effect, to go one last time to Sonya, that fragile being, who represents the starting point of his trial, and from whom he is to take up the cross. There, as previously, he talks, she listens; although it was she who had instructed him—prior to Porfiry's doing so—that he must confess, if he is to live. Porfiry rationalizes it in base psychological terms, self-consciously and awkwardly, as though finding himself misplaced at a pulpit (*"You can't get on without us* . . . .Because suffering . . . is a great thing . . . "* 442). Sonya, in dual contrast, expresses the same idea naturally and instinctively in purely mystical terms, *feeling* the truth of her words, which are communicated—and ultimately received—as such.

"Go at once, this instant, stand at the cross-roads, first bow down and kiss the earth you have desecrated, then bow to the whole world, to the four corners of the earth, and say aloud to all the world: 'I have done murder.' Then God will send you life again." (403)

At the close, it is her words that he will enact as deed after symbolically taking up the cross, and will remember as hers at the moment of their enactment—as transformation from spirit to flesh—which testifies to their profound significance for him.

> He had suddenly remembered Sonya's words: "Go to the cross-roads; bow down before the people, and kiss the ground, because you are guilty before them, and say aloud to all the world, 'I am a murderer'." (505)

Thus we read that, at the moment prior to his bowing to the ground and kissing the earth, Raskolnikov had remembered Sonya's words, whose forceful significance compels him to fall to his knees in penance. However, although placed in quotation marks, they are not hers—not precisely hers; nor are they his, to be sure, since the point of origin of his reported (inner) speech is, indeed, her previous entreaty. These imprecisely recollected words belong in fact to no one as specific author, but exist, again, on the borders of dialogue—between murderer and harlot, atheist and believer, sinner and victim. They are, then, purely dialogical—and perfectly suited to convey the verbal message that inspires their complementary dramatic enactment.

As a concluding paradoxical point, the characters' speech, their inclusive dialogues, and the several forms of report initially outlined as model to contain those dialogues are all structurally indeterminate in analogous fashion. The boundaries between the latter (from, say, the minimal to partial report) shift at the mere inclusion of a single word as reported speech. That speech, in turn, may clearly exist on the borders of its various users' utterances (as quasi-direct speech). Moreover, a speech event within one dialogue may, as just noted, have its dramatic manifestation or ramification within another "frame" entirely. Hence the strangely rewarding process of seeking after boundaries where—one instinctively knows—there are none.

As a final such instance, Porfiry asks Raskolnikov at their first meeting whether he believes *literally* in the raising of Lazarus. He responds hesitantly that he does. But later, at his subsequent meeting with Sonya, he requests that she read the passage—and then marvels at her joyous faith in the Word, which he presumably does not share.

> "Well, there it is!" ["Nu, tak i est'!"] he thought.
>
> . . . .
>
> "That's it, that's it!" ["Tak i est'! tak i est'!" VI,248]
> he repeated to himself, insistently. (311)
>
> . . . .
>
> Raskolnikov turned and looked at her with emotion:
> Yes, that was it! (314) [Da, tak i est'! VI,251]

Although not attributed as such, that concluding *apparent* authorial phrase, an exultant affirmation of Sonya as *yurodivaya*, is originally employed by Raskolnikov (twice), and belongs, then, not to the author as source but to his character. As an instance of unacknowledged (or "unreported") reported speech (that is, quasi-direct discourse), the phrase is "borrowed," as it were, for its effective repeated epithet-like quality, illustrating yet another case of reported speech existing on the boundaries of narrative discourse, of which it is a virtually indispensable component.

Although Raskolnikov declares his faith to Porfiry, he comports himself to the contrary in his talks with Sonya. He thus confirms her apperception of him, expressed in her own mystical terms ("And *he, he* who is also blind and unbelieving . . ."), while at the same time she affirms her own unquestioning faith—

> . . . he also will hear in a moment, he also will believe.
> Yes, yes! Here and now! (314)

Hence the motivation behind her reading for *him* to hear *now*. And, although her belief that the Biblical passage will serve as the immediate catalyst for his spiritual awakening is premature and unfounded, that she herself will serve gradually in that same crucial capacity is certain. For in more complex analogue to the parable, and in greater tortuous manner, she will emerge as the source of light that will summon the dead from the darkness of the cave. Yet in the world of the novel, as the author himself implies at the end, the process inevitably takes time.

5

Dialogic Thematics

The Brothers Karamazov

Highly syncretic in conception, Dostoevsky's last work differs greatly in structure from those that preceded it. The exceptional use of heterogeneous material incorporated within its framework is one register of that difference. Narrative forms including folklore legends, saints' lives, Biblical tales, apocrypha, and various anecdotes are related at various stages throughout. These narrative forms are an integral part of the fabric of the novel, meriting attention as such and for their prominent role in supporting or refuting its contending ideas. They will therefore be given their due in the present chapter.

The great proliferation and density of distinct, miniature narrative forms within the novel may be immediately demonstrated. First, the two central chapters of Book Five ("Rebellion," "The Grand Inquisitor") and the entire central chapter of Book Six ("Notes of the Life of the Elder Zosima . . ."), together forming the ideological core of the novel, are constructed from such narrative forms. In addition, a whole series of isolated chapters either focus on a recollected anecdote or tale, which functions as its central unifying device, or are structured as a string of such miniature narratives. These chapters include: "Stinking Lizaveta," "The Controversy," "An Onion," "Mitya's Great Secret. Received with Hisses," "Peasant Women Who Have Faith," "The Confession of an Ardent Heart—

in Anecdotes," "Kolya Krasotkin," "The Lost Dog," "The Medical Experts and a Pound of Nuts." Second, most of the novel's major and minor characters recite anecdotes of varying length, and thus assume the role of secondary narrator for some fraction of the book. The novel's "storytellers" are the following: Fedor Pavlovich, Ivan, Dmitry, Zosima, Grushenka, Katerina Ivanovna, Captain Snegirev, the peasant women who have faith, Miusov, Fetyukovich, Kolya Krasotkin, Doctor Gertsenshtube, Liza Khokhlakova, Father Ferapont, the devil, Pan Vrublevsky, Maksimov, and Dmitry's peasant coachman on the road to Mokroe. Finally, anecdotes are related about virtually every character of the novel as well—making them, in a whole series of instances, either the subject or teller of the tale, or both. The subjects of the novel's miniature stories are these: Fedor Pavlovich, his two older sons, his two wives, Smerdyakov, Lizaveta, the two women of the novel, Captain Snegirev, Ilyusha, the latter's dog, Kolya Krasotkin, the servant Grigory and his six fingered infant, the monks at Mount Athos, elders, various saints and the Virgin Mary.

These blanket observations necessarily lead to a series of interrelated questions. How are we to account, first of all, for this proliferation of story forms generated from a multitude of viewpoints? How do the various accounts serve to reveal the network of relationships involved? And, how does this complex narrative technique serve as an ordering principle, making of the novel a cohesive, integrated work, rather than a dissociated thing?

In broad terms, it will be the aim of this chapter to show that certain narrative portions of the text may be isolated according to a specific fixed schema, or model, and analyzed in relation to the greater narrative of which it is a part. Such distinct, easily isolated passages, representing independently organized story forms within the greater text, will here be considered as a form of "subtext." For present purposes, all instances of these may be viewed as constituting a hypothetical secondary plane of the novel. In contrast, those elements of the story which make up the main plot—centering on the killing of the father and the role of each of the sons—will be considered the novel's primary plane of action. Between the two planes there is a constant "dialogue," as will be shown. By positing two narrative planes superimposed one upon the other, and supposing in the process a limited hierarchical ordering to the structure of the novel, the miniature narratives of the secondary will be seen to support and give rise to the development of plot and idea on the primary. This, in essence, sums up the present intent, which is to show the interconnectedness and interdependence between the two levels posited (or between the part and the whole), whereby oppositions and meaning are generated, while opposing philosophical positions are revealed and maintained.

As a distinct, delimited form, the subtext may be conceived as a narrative unit relating a self-contained story of its own. It is concerned with the depiction of events outside the temporal and spatial boundaries of the novel proper or main plot. The event depicted, having occurred earlier than the time span covered by the main plot, causes a displacement within the greater narrative's temporal plane which allows for its expansion and inclusion of other synchronic elements. Similarly, there is a frequent corresponding displacement within the novel's spatial plane to some setting other than that of the primary events. While sidetracking the main course of events, the subtext nevertheless comments upon them as well. This is what makes it significant and worthy of consideration. The subtext may thus be considered an "additional" synchronic element cast upon the syntagmatic axis, where it functions as a device of retardation. At the same time it illuminates the ideological positions and corresponding psychological features of the individual characters espousing those positions.

The subtext enters the novel according to either the principle of contiguity or similarity—and thus stands in either a metonymic or metaphoric relationship to the novel's main plot.

Correspondingly, the intended generic notion of "subtext" must be understood in terms of two related but distinct types, designated an "anecdote" and "incorporated tale." In brief, the former refers to narratives which have to do with the world of the Karamazovs, which is the world of the novel proper, and may therefore be regarded as being contiguous to that world. By contrast, the incorporated tales are accounts drawn from outside the realm of the novel, but which have their analogue within its greater story. Other features apply as follows.

The anecdote, as noted, always relates an incident from an earlier period than that covered by the time span of the novel proper and is usually set elsewhere from the principal narrative which it invariably interrupts. But while the anecdote always represents a shift in perspective, it is always elucidative rather than extraneous or digressive, and provides either some striking unexpected perspective to one of the novel's main figures or events, or establishes some basic opposition or parallel. Characterized by its brevity and relative isolation from other plot components (since it marks a break in the story line), the anecdote describes an occurrence which was completed sometime in the past; in this respect, it is analogous to the perfective aspect of the Russian verb. The habitual does not make for an anecdote; only the single unique occurrence told as a story, however sparing in detail, is representative of the form.

Thus Smerdyakov's childhood pastime of hanging cats with pomp and circumstance is only mentioned as the peculiar practice of a strange child ("Smerdyakov"), but is not related in the form of an isolated narrative depicting an individual occurrence, and must therefore be considered a detail of characterization of another order from the anecdote as here defined. On the other hand, the story of the precocious Kolya Krasotkin's making himself prone along the railroad tracks to await an oncoming train, and thus demonstrating his courage to boys older than he, is representative of a single incident related in story form. The same may be said of the account of the six-fingered infant born to the servant Grigory and of his intransigent view of it ("a dragon"), or of Fedor Pavlovich's nocturnal encounter with the idiot girl Lizaveta, and of numerous other instances in the novel—all of which occurred "earlier and (frequently) elsewhere" from the main plot. The anecdote is thus an extended part of the story proper. It is a part of the world of the novel to the extent that it touches upon the principal characters and their milieu. It may therefore be said to enter the novel on the principle of contiguity, as a source of new, and often crucial, information—which thus testifies to the vitality of this small story form within the overall structure of which it is a part.

In contrast to the anecdote which is in essence a part of the story of the novel, the incorporated tale is one which is drawn from either a fictive or documentable source outside the realm of the novel proper. It is, in fact, an incorporated text, examples of which include the many folklore legends, excerpts from saints' lives, apocryphal and Biblical tales excerpted in the novel, the newspaper account which sparks the discussion at Fedor Pavlovich's ("The Controversy"), and Ivan's novella, "The Grand Inquisitor".[1] All of these incorporated tales are derived from sources outside the novel (whether fictive or true being irrelevant to our schema), but are made to function in a definite, fully determinate manner within its context. In short, they parallel, reflect, parody, or model the two fundamentally opposed ideas of the novel, and thus create a network of relationships which link the various narrative accounts, stories, and tales to one another, and to the text as a whole.

In all instances, the incorporated tale enters the novel on the principle of similarity. Because it invariably models the very text of which it is a part, it is an iconic structure. Likewise, many of the novel's anecdotes, although entering the text according to the principle of contiguity, also function iconically. Both categories of subtext are thus related in this respect as well. Further, as a commonly held point of view, affirming the mimetic function of art, the novel, as a finite artifact, is seen to model an infinite universe. It is our contention here that the subtexts of the novel at hand, in analogous fashion, model the world of the Karamazovs within an extensive internal modeling system, which is central to the composition of the work and which justifies our initial observation that Dostoevsky's last novel is structured in very different, vastly more intricate fashion than his earlier works.

While the incorporated tale may of course possess an immanent aesthetic value of its own, it derives its meaning within the primary text to the degree that it serves as parallel to it or is reflective of it. Grushenka's story of the onion, for example, easily lends itself to an analysis of the parallels it establishes with the main story of the novel. Her account tells of an old woman condemned to eternal flames. Feeling compassion for the woman, an angel offers her a chance to attain salvation by allowing her to catch hold of an onion and be pulled from the burning lake. When other condemned souls try to hold onto her and be saved as well, she cruelly fends them off, loses her grip, and falls back into the inferno.

The story offers, first, a reverse mirror effect of the situation between Alesha and Grushenka, for which it serves as metaphor. The old lady of the tale represents the counter example to Grushenka, whose unexpected human concern for Alesha marks the beginning of the process of release from her anguish and suffering of the past five years. In marked contrast to the teller of the tale, the old lady—by not having attained spiritual insight from the mercy shown her, and by refusing to show pity for others—remains condemned. In this respect, her situation parallels that of Ivan and Katerina Ivanovna, who have also failed individually to gain new insights, and whose suffering is therefore also left unrelieved. Thus, in terms of the novel's governing ethic—that suffering is borne until one recognizes the fundamental responsibility each has for all—a clear rationale exists for the continued torment of the old woman of the tale and, contrastively, for Grushenka's own release. An integrated part of the novel, then, not only for its thematic parallels, her tale also bears an ideational component inherently linked to one of the novel's principal dialectics. Moreover, her telling of the tale is pivotal, since it provides a source of mutual understanding between her and Alesha, by which the apparent opposition between "saint" and "sinner" is formidably reduced—through the novel's same governing dialectic illustrated by the tale. Finally, in concentrating upon the problem of suffering, the story is thematically related to the other incorporated tales of the novel, all of which are concerned with the same problem.[2]

In assessing the role of the tale incorporated into the greater text of the novel, Voloshinov's observations regarding reported speech again yield striking parallels. He defines his subject in the following well-known formulation: "Reported speech is speech within speech, utterance within utterance, and at the same time also *speech about speech, utterance about utterance*" (1973:115). The incorporated tale may be described in analogous terms as a self-contained unit within the greater story, which, like reported speech, also represents a kind of indirect or oblique discourse, commenting upon the novel's principal themes posed within its primary plane. Integrated into the narrative flow as the discourse of a given character, the tale is designed to establish a clear analogy between its subject and the overall text of which it is a part. There is always some kind of linkage or connection, in other words, between the stories told by the characters and the story told by the novelist.

Further analogies apply as well between reported speech and the incorporated tale, when Voloshinov observes that "Between the reported speech and the reporting context, dynamic relations of high complexity and tension are in force. . . . The reported speech and the reporting context are but the terms of a dynamic relationship" (Ibid.:119). This abstract formulation is similarly relevant to the structure of *The Brothers*, where there is a like dynamic reciprocal relationship in effect. For the tales of the novel document, substantiate, and dramatize the philosophical positions of the novel's two principal theoreticians, Ivan and Zosima. To the former are attributed tales which are meant to demonstrate injustice in the world; to the latter belong stories suggesting that injustice may be rectified only through an individual's spontaneous recognition of spiritual values. Hence the tales are the ideas of the novel given dramatic substance; they are the miniature prisms through which the novel's ideas are fragmented, refracted, and realized in aesthetic form.

*

There are two fundamentally opposed ideas in *The Brothers*, to which all others are subordinated, and from whose perspective the novel's subtexts may be understood in relation to one another and to the principal ideas themselves. Ivan's notion that "everything is permitted" a presumably superior individual who, in the absence of God, may allow himself the freedom to act according to his own amoral plan is countered by Zosima's view that "each is responsible to everyone for everyone and everything." The two ideas reflect diametrically opposed philosophical approaches to the world: its joyful acceptance and its outright "rejection"—on the grounds that inexplicable cruelty and horror are all too evident constitutive features. Each idea is articulated and vitalized in a series of related instances by its principal adherents or detractors. In addition, they find implicit expression in encapsulated monadic form as the subtexts of the novel (as in Grushenka's tale)— themselves expressive by virtue of their artistic conception and incorporation within the text as other than blatant philosophical formulation.

The novel offers, then, on the two planes designated as primary and secondary, the confrontation of a Christian vision by an atheistic view, the one espousing man's responsibility to man as members of a single human community, the other denying the existence of any moral design to the universe and man's place within it. This fundamental opposition gives form to the main ideological conception of the novel, and is meant to be taken here as the matrix of its hierarchically organized contrapuntal structure. Of the novel's two governing ideas, Zosima's is consistently expounded through sympathetic spokesmen, primarily Alesha, who continues to propagate the teachings of his mentor; the other, contrastively, is related through a series of antipathetic viewpoints, culminating in that expressed by Ivan's devil and leading ultimately to the idea's deterioration in the mind of its author. It is the elaboration of the latter theory that will receive our primary attention, and it is to its initial formulation within the pages of *The Brothers* that we turn now.

The Idea Expounded. Miusov and Ivan.

During the scene in the elder's cell ("An Unfortunate Gathering"), numerous tales and anecdotes are related in seemingly innocent manner. Yet the aim of each teller is to pique some other (family) member present. Thus Fedor Pavlovich's brother-in-law, Miusov, requests the company's indulgence that he might recount a "slight anecdote" (*malen'kij anekdot*) based upon his meeting in Paris with a police official. The latter had spoken of the anarchists, atheists, and various revolutionary types who provided him with a career. His words are reported by Miusov.

> We keep watch on them and know all their goings-on.
> But there are a few peculiar men among them who
> believe in God and are Christians, but at the same time
> are socialists. Those are the people we are most afraid

> of. They are dreadful people! The socialist who is a
> Christian is more to be dreaded than a socialist who is
> an atheist. (58)

The thrust of those words is directed at Ivan, who, in the course
of events, will be shown to exhibit precisely that duality which
Miusov's police official designates as belonging to the "socialist
who is a Christian" (*socialist-xristianin*). When Ivan speaks of
his rejection of the current order ("Rebellion") in favor of a
utopian ideal ("The Grand Inquisitor"), the "socialist" aspect is
revealed. The "Christian" facet is made most evident in the
poignant scenes where he is shown wrestling with the problem
of faith ("The Devil. Ivan Fedorovich's Nightmare"). Moreover, Ivan's admission to Alesha—"Well, just imagine, perhaps
I too accept God . . . " (215)—would again confirm that he is
indeed related to the type specified by Miusov, whose pointed
epigrammatic account captures the essential feature of Ivan's
duality, which is first gradually, and then climactically, revealed. At the same time, the account also formulates in bare
succinct form the inner struggle between atheistic and Christian precepts with which the novel as a whole is concerned.

Once again in the cell, Miusov takes the floor and makes
Ivan the object of his remarks, more blatantly, when he recounts directly in deprecating tones the main thrust of Ivan's
ideas. On this occasion, Ivan intimates a certain aggressiveness
on the part of the prideful intellectual, which nevertheless
remains muted in the cell, only to appear full blown in the
tavern ("Rebellion").

> I will tell you, gentlemen, another extremely interest-
> ing and most characteristic anecdote of Ivan
> Fedorovich himself. Only five days ago, in a gathering
> here, principally of ladies, he solemnly declared in
> argument that there was nothing in the whole world
> to make men love their neighbors. That there was no
> law of nature that man should love mankind, and that,

if there had been any love on earth hitherto, it was not owing to a natural law, but simply because men have believed in immortality. Ivan Fedorovich added in parenthesis that the whole natural law lies in that faith, and that if you were to destroy in mankind the belief in immortality, not only love but every living force maintaining the life of the world would at once be dried up. Moreover, nothing then would be immoral, everything would be lawful, even cannibalism. That's not all. He ended by asserting that for every individual, like ourselves, who does not believe in God or immortality, the moral law of nature must immediately be changed into the exact contrary of the former religious law, and that egoism, even unto crime, must become, not only lawful but even recognized as the inevitable, the most rational, even honorable outcome of his position. From this paradox, gentlemen, you can judge of the rest of our eccentric and paradoxical friend Ivan Fedorovich's theories. (60)

Thus is Ivan's theory summed up. Couched in language and tone suggestive of an inconceivable, thoroughly extreme point of view, the stature of the idea is clearly diminished by its being ridiculed by a speaker intent upon discrediting it. Rather than be given direct expression by its principal exponent, Ivan's theory is relegated to what has here been designated the novel's secondary plane, where it is summarily expressed as an anecdote. The point of view chosen for its formulation and expression is not only unsympathetic but anticipatory of the idea's eventual foreclosure. Thus, while pointing to characteristic features of Ivan (his great intellectual ability matched by a high degree of egotism), his capitulation as ideologist is prepared for by a narrative technique that allows for his idea to be initially presented in such deprecating manner.[3] Employment of the device is consistent and uniform throughout. Ironic elaboration of the idea in the cell foreshadows its ultimate collapse when filtered through the devil as instrument for its final negative critique.

As the single prior instance, Miusov's initial account prepares for the idea's thorough discrediting by the time of its second and final telling. His use of the term "anecdote" is noteworthy, since it bears (in the Russian) the connotation of a light-hearted account. That connotation runs counter, of course, to Ivan's intentions, imbued within his (reported) speech, but affirms Miusov's antagonistic position from the start. The latter emphasizes that Ivan presented his notion "in the presence of ladies," an intentionally unflattering detail, suggesting a certain indelicacy, compounded by Ivan's reportedly triumphant manner. Miusov's general characterization of both the idea and its author signals an intention diametrically opposed to that originally intended. The entire account is couched in language and tone meant to suggest a thoroughly untenable point of view, whose potential stature is immediately diminished by its being contemptuously related by an antagonist intent upon discrediting it.

Introduced by a pair of ironic superlatives ("extremely interesting and most characteristic") and sustained corresponding intonation, Ivan's idea is characterized as inconceivable and utterly indefensible, allowing for grotesque possibility ("even cannibalism; egoism, even unto crime"). Indications of such extreme viewpoint are present throughout Miusov's brief account, where the language attributed to Ivan brooks no dispute or possible qualifying detail ("there was nothing in the whole world; there was no law; the whole natural law; every living force; would at once be dried up; nothing then would be immoral; everything would be lawful; for every individual; must immediately be changed; must become; the inevitable, the most rational . . . outcome . . . "). The idea is thus summed up by a speaker, who imbues the account not only with his own intentions (to disparage the idea, to denigrate its author) and ironic intonation but with his own speech, incorporated to indicate feigned surprise and mock indignation ("Moreover . . . That's not all; even . . . even . . . even; From this paradox . . . you can judge . . . our eccentric and paradoxical friend . . . ").

In Miusov's view, Ivan does not speak; he pontificates. This impression is also conveyed in Miusov's choice of expression ("he solemnly declared; Ivan Fedorovich added in parenthesis; he ended by asserting"). His concluding, falsely endearing epithets ("our . . . friend") soften neither the effect nor the characterization (of either the author or his idea). Thus Dmitry's excited request for further clarification is immediately inspired: "If I've heard right: crime must not only be permitted but even recognized as the inevitable and the most rational outcome of his position for every atheist!" (60). This is followed by Dmitry's telling remark: "I will remember," a prominent false lead, since the idea is not his to act upon (or guide others)—but will later appear so. His outburst parallels Razumikhin's similarly voiced disbelief (cited earlier) in *Crime and Punishment*; in the two respective instances, Ivan's brother and Raskolnikov's friend fulfill the same compositional need: to sound an immediate alarm at what is being articulated.

In the presentation of Ivan's idea, only a single laconic statement in the entire novel can be directly attributed to him (as other than reported speech or that of an alter ego), which he makes in response to Zosima: "There is no virtue if there is no immortality" (60). By contrast to such paucity of direct speech on the part of the author of the idea, the clearly unsympathetic point of view chosen for its initial formulation and expression— paralleling Porfiry's similar presentation in *Crime and Punishment*—is itself anticipatory of the idea's eventual foreclosure. No less than Raskolnikov's, Ivan's capitulation as ideologist is prepared for by the device which allows his theory to be presented in such deprecating manner. In contrastive tones, the elder Zosima observes with sympathy and perspicuity: "The question is still fretting your heart, and is not answered. . . . Meanwhile, in your despair, you, too, divert yourself . . . though you don't believe your own arguments, and with an aching heart mock at them inwardly . . . .That question you have not answered, and it is your great grief, for it clamors for an answer" (61). The dramatic manifestation of that accurate and prophetic remark left open (as the final ellipses here signify) is realized only at the end of the novel during the confrontation between Ivan and that part of himself which "mocks inwardly."

Kolya and Ivan.

Ivan's position is discredited by other techniques as well. A critical commonplace regarding *The Brothers* is that the world of the children represents a special analogue to the adult world of the Karamazovs; what figures there has its counterpart in that of the children. Within this framework, the precocious Kolya Krasotkin and the proud intellectual, Ivan Karamazov, are related character types. The former, as an adolescent representation of the latter, may be viewed as a mirror image offering another perspective from which to regard Ivan. Much of what is still blatant in the adolescent's psychology is more subtly hidden in the adult's; thus the former provides a key to the latter. Such key, representing one of the subtexts of the novel, centers on an absurd grotesque that Kolya is nevertheless anxious to relate. Although unobtrusive, its significance is made evident by an elaborate series of references made prior to its telling which is thereby thoroughly anticipated.[4]

Kolya relates how he had once walked through the marketplace with an errand boy. Having observed a goose stretching its neck under the rear wheel of a cart to get at a few grains, he suggests that if the cart were to be moved forward a bit, its neck would be broken. The idea is immediately put into action by his companion, and the truth of the propositon is irrefutably demonstrated. At the same moment, an outcry is raised by the peasants in the stalls who had witnessed the deed, and the two boys are taken to court. There Kolya defends himself by "coldly" asserting: "I simply stated the general proposition, had spoken hypothetically" (518). The episode concludes with the errand boy obliged to pay and Kolya released with a reprimand from the court.

Although the story represents only a minimal aspect of the novel's greater plan, it reflects in parodic miniature the highly complex relationship between Ivan and Smerdyakov. Moreover, what gradually comes to light during the three interviews is simply blurted out by Kolya when brought to court as no more than a naive defense. By regarding the characters of the anecdote as purely compositional elements in the respective roles of mentor, disciple, and victim, the tale may be seen to function as part of an internal modeling system reflecting in microcosm the much larger problem of the novel as a whole, erupting in the murder of Fedor Pavlovich. Such modeling system thus extends far beyond the little tale just cited and beyond the world of the children. In terms of mentor-disciple relationships, as a prominent case in point, Ivan is Smerdyakov's authority, while the latter teaches Ilyusha the art of cruelty (the story of the lost dog). Similarly, Zosima is Alesha's spiritual guide, while the young novice fulfills a like role with regard to Kolya and the other boys. Yet Ivan, too, has a decided influence on Kolya. All such relationships are thus reminiscent of the effect produced in a hall of mirrors, as each reflects back on the others. This same effect is worked out at the ideological core of the novel as well—by the juxtaposition of the novel's subtexts and the responsive points of view elicited and variously expressed.

Smerdyakov and Ivan.

The most crucial mentor-disciple relationship of the novel is that of Ivan and Smerdyakov. It provides the pivot upon which

the ideational and thematic axes of the novel turn. That
Smerdyakov's fate hinges on Ivan's acceptance or rejection of
moral responsibility for the crime remains a commonplace view.
Likewise, in terms of plot contingencies and ideational plan, his
suicide is requisite to the working out of the novel's whole
design. The question of how Smerdyakov's suicide is motivated
is therefore pertinent. Although there are great social and
economic differences separating the half-brothers, it is rather
a metaphysical difference underlying all others that determines why the one is wholly condemned, while the other is left
in a precarious state of mental imbalance, from which he may
well recover, but will never be the same. To understand what
makes for Smerdyakov's alienation and suicide, the nature of
his atheistic view may be considered in light of Ivan's. For there
is a critical difference in the fact that the convictions of the one
are self-imposed or self-taught, while the limitations of the
other constitute a peculiar deficiency in nature. How this distinction is realized in artistic form and conveyed to the reader
is detailed as part of the novel's secondary plane, wherein the
highly informative subtext bears the semantic weight.

Through the medium of two anecdotes related in immediate
succession, concerning Smerdyakov when still a youth, a
peculiar characteristic of the future lackey and murderer is
momentarily brought to light. First, the reader learns that
Smerdyakov's religious instruction under the tutelage of the
servant Grigory had come to a precipitous end. The pupil had
quickly displayed a disdainful regard for what he was being
taught, and balked at the start. ("God created light on the first
day, and the sun, moon, and stars on the fourth day. Where did
the light come from on the first day?" 112). A sharp slap in the
face from the distraught servant concludes the matter. In this
instance, the encounter between potential mentor and disciple
represents in parodic form but one in the long series of confrontations between atheist and believer, culminating in the far
more crucial complex of relations and oppositions at the novel's

ideological core (Books Five and Six). In the second instance, which is said to have occurred several years after the first, the reader learns of the youth's quick disenchantment with Gogol's *Dikanka* stories ("It's all untrue" 113). Neither literature nor the Bible, it seems, has any meaning for this prosaic, pedestrian mentality. What the two anecdotes show is that the realm of symbolic significance or metaphor is impenetrable for Smerdyakov, who operates solely on the level of the concrete implementation of an idea. One which cannot be implemented in mundane reality has no reality for him. Thus are the distressingly narrow confines of his world delimited.

This conception of Smerdyakov's terribly restricted vision, from which is precluded the possibility of even conceiving of a transcendent metaphysical plane, is substantiated later by the discussion at Fedor Pavlovich's. The "controversy" there, focusing on a tale of a soldier who submits to torture and death at the hands of Asiatics rather than renounce his Christian faith, resembles in its basic motifs the crowning episode from a traditional saint's life. Once again Smerdyakov antagonizes Grigory who finds the account edifying. By means of his own warped casuistry, the lackey aims to show that the soldier would have done better to renounce his faith, and later devote the remainder of his life to doing penitence through good works. By virtue of his own natural limitations, Grigory is unable to formulate a counter argument to the view propagated by the cleverer Smerdyakov. In this instance, again, the views of atheist and believer are rendered mutually exclusive.

Hence all of these accounts prepare for the later, fuller development of the same theme: the atheist's "literal" conception of the world based on his own cognitive powers, opposed by the symbolic perception of the believer. In the episode dealing with the controversy, moreover, the tale itself, as the nucleus or main focus of the discussion, represents a kind of "pro and contra" encompassing in microcosm the greater problem of the novel as a whole—the opposition of atheism to Christianity—

which characterizes both the theme of the tale itself and the kind of polarity elicited by it in the subsequent discussion. What transpires during the controversy—as Smerdyakov promotes an all too convenient, temporary rejection of one's faith and principles—anticipates the lackey's later reception and implementation of Ivan's theory, which demands a self-serving amoral vision entirely undiluted by any conception of a higher ideal. At this early stage, there is only the veiled suggestion of a potential partnership, but Smerdyakov holds forth his views in great enough detail here for the reader to recognize later in this mean shallow mind not only the ability to convert an abstract theoretical statement into a literal edict sanctioning murder—but his inability to do otherwise. Made evident by the novel's subtexts, it is therefore the lackey alone in whom is incarnate the "atheist par excellence," as a type incapable of conceptualizing a transcendent ideal.

In stark contrast, assuming the intellectual stance of one who has arrived at a decision and is determined to stand by it, Ivan declares to Alesha:

> I understand nothing . . . I don't want to understand anything now. I want to stick to the fact. I made up my mind long ago not to understand. If I try to understand anything, I shall be false to the fact and I have determined to stick to the fact. (224)

Ivan's determination "not to understand" signifies his conscious intent to reject steadfastly any conception of the transcendent, with its attendant symbolic modes of conceptualization. He is determined not to allow himself the "luxury" of a symbolic interpretation of reality, which represents to him an all too comfortable rationale for the existing evil in the world. Ivan's is a considered decision to reject the symbolic in favor of the literal, the transcendent for the real, since he is unable to conceive of a rational means for their synthesis. In effect, he places his trust in the cognitive powers given to man, which enable him to report objectively the brutal details of existence, but not to penetrate to their ultimate meaning. Ivan is thus intent upon cultivating a "rational" approach to the apprehension of phenomena, "to stick to the fact." He can conceive of a Euclidean universe defined by three dimensions, and will therefore credit the resultant formulations of Euclidean geometry, as he acknowledges to Alesha. But since he cannot apprehend the underlying principles of non-Euclidean geometry, he will not accept its ramifications. ("Even if parallel lines do meet and I see it myself, I shall see it and say that they've met, but still I won't accept it. That's what's at the root of me, Alesha; that's my thesis." 217). The flaw in his argument, of course, lies in his reduction of phenomena to match his own intellectual capacities. By measuring the world exclusively according to his own abilities to perceive, Ivan sacrifices a potentially broader conception of the universe for a simpler subjective vision. His "rebellion" reduces, then, to the desire for a world tailor-made to his understanding.

In the case of Smerdyakov, the very possibility of his consciously rejecting the symbolic plane of interpretation is precluded by his limited vision devoid of the faculty for perceiving it. This limitation separates him from Ivan and leads ultimately to suicide as the alternative and likely culmination to an abortive career. Yet at the same time, Ivan and Smerdyakov share a basic affinity which makes for their strange communion: both are in a state of mutiny. Smerdyakov's paltry rebellion is lodged against his abject and lowly place in the established social order. ("Grigory Vasilevich blames me for rebelling against my birth . . . but I would have sanctioned their killing me before I was born that I might not have come into the world at all . . . " 206). Ivan rages against the moral order, and means to buttress his argument with tangible evidence. To this end he brings to bear his collection of cruel anecdotes and tales about child torturers, Turkish atrocities, execution and murder.

Ivan opens his case for rebellion by recalling an account drawn from a saint's life.

> I once read somewhere of "John the Merciful," a saint, that when a hungry, frozen beggar came to him, and asked him to warm him up, he took him into his bed, held him in his arms, and began breathing into his mouth, which was putrid and loathsome from some awful disease. I am convinced that he did that from the laceration of falsity, for the sake of the love imposed by duty, as a penance laid on him. (218)

But his interpretation is directly opposed to the one intended. For rather than acknowledge the story as being illustrative of the Christian ideal of exhibiting brotherly love, Ivan reduces it with his seemingly keen psychological dialectic to a perverse act on the part of the ascetic. Thus Ivan denies what Smerdyakov cannot help but deny. Unlike the lackey, Ivan is fully capable of grasping the symbolic import of the naturalistic detail, but intentionally draws a conclusion opposed to the spirit of the tale. As a form of intellectual perversity, characterized by the very unwillingness to acknowledge what is fully comprehended, the interpretation that Ivan chooses to place on the episode is worthy only of his baser instincts—embodied in Smerdyakov, his lower self and condemned alter ego.

Ivan and Zosima.

In Books Five and Six of the novel, the concentration of subtexts reaches its highest density, testifying to their important role within the work's ideational stratum—itself predominant in this central part of the novel to the virtual exclusion of plot. Although the book's principal ideas are conveyed through both dialogic (Ivan and Alesha at the tavern) and monologic form (Alesha's biographical "Notes" on the life and works of his elder), the subtext (as anecdote and incorporated tale) is uniformly employed as the device by which the ideas are vitalized and dramatized, and thus removed from the realm of philosophic discourse to that of aesthetic, narrative form. The limited aim here will be to show how these story forms or narrative units are juxtaposed along various related axes of meaning to either support or refute the novel's contending ideas.

Ivan is not given to express his theory directly; however he does bring to bear a substantial number of "little facts and anecdotes" (*faktiki* and *anekdotiki*), which he utilizes to document what he conceives to be the senseless horror of the existential order. In taking the offensive against the bastions of faith represented by his brother, Ivan's tales of cruelty and suffering, of murder and the guillotine, lend his position stature and power. The desired effect is achieved in part by virtue of their inherent dramatic qualities, coupled with shock value, and in part as a result of Ivan's own direct telling and developing of his argument (his shrill tone notwithstanding), in contradistinction to the presentation of his theory, which is consistently relegated to indirect and clearly unsympathetic accounts (Miusov, the devil). In short, the problem reduces to that of point of view and the limited extent to which Ivan is allowed to express his views (as direct speech), as opposed to their being formulated by some other, deprecating voice. The degree to which Ivan's position is elaborated by its author, in other words, is directly related to its ultimate stature within the ideational framework of the text.

Zosima's ideas are also expressed indirectly—by Alesha, who serves as biographer and amanuensis. Both philosophies are thus revealed by characters other than their respective authors. Yet, in striking contrast, the same device ensures that Zosima's views be conveyed from a wholly sympathetic standpoint as a collection of "teachings" (a term already bearing a distinctly positive connotation). Another important shared

feature, both ideological positions are presented in like manner—
by the incorporation of a series of subtexts, which "ground" the
idea in much the same relationship as the signifier (form)
stands to signified (concept), according to the conventionally
accepted notion of sign theory. Ivan has his gruesome tales to
support his views; Zosima, his biographically derived anecdotes.
It is not a lack, then, of dramatic documentation which emerges
as the significant differentiating factor in the presentation of
the novel's contending viewpoints. Rather, it is the perspective
from which an idea is propounded, which in the end distinguishes the two positions and prefigures the outcome of their
contention.

Another pronounced difference, the stories recounted by
Ivan (incorporated tales, by definition, within our schema) do
not relate directly to either the teller or his world. In this sense,
they contrast with the anecdotes bearing on Zosima's early
career, which are more closely bound to the elder as intimate
revelations. The fact that Ivan's morbid accounts lack this
positive feature serves to distance further the reader from Ivan
and his theory—from which the latter, too, seems distanced by
virtue of Miusov's negative truncated account's being the only
one presented (prior to the devil's final devastating summation).
Ivan's theory, moreover, appears inorganic and artificial—as a
notion arrived at by concentrated cerebration rather than em-
pirical understanding—in contrast to the organic spiritual
development experienced by Zosima, and revealed in his
stories.

Having, in any case, determined "to stick with the fact,"
Ivan utilizes his collection of ostensible, cold hard facts to
substantiate his negation of the moral order. Ivan's rejection of
"God's world" ("in the final result I don't accept this world of
God's, and, although I know it exists, I don't accept it at all"
216) is developed precisely through the integration of the subtext (as incorporated tale) into his argument, making it far less
abstract by lending it dramatic substance. As the case in point,

the chapter, "Rebellion," composed partly of tales and partly of philosophical argumentation, may thus be described as a structure in which the tale, a narrative unit incorporated within the secondary plane of the novel, is at the same time integrated within the novel's governing ideational stratum. The result is a structural bond emanating from the interdependency between the incorporated tale, which finds its raison d'être (as part of the novel) in the idea to be documented or substantiated—and of the latter being made concrete through the supportive presence of the former. In semiotic terms, the tale may be understood as form (signifier) bearing no inherent value of its own within the text except in relation to a specific concept (signified): the idea in the novel to which it refers.[5] In this sense, the subtext is again seen to function as part of an internal modeling system, which is especially prominent within the novel's ideational core.

Such generic bond, in which narrative is irrevocably bound to ideational content, may be viewed as a model for describing the structure of the entire novel, itself wholly ideational in its conception. For every idea finds its dramatization on some level of the novel, either as part of the primary plot, or as a subtext displaced from the principal story to a secondary level of narration, or as a dream ("The Babe"), vision ("Cana of Galilee"), or hallucination ("Ivan Fedorovich's Nightmare. The Devil")—all of which function to encapsulate the greater concerns of the novel in some smaller form, as highly distinct narrative units within the overall plot.

This same bond of inherent mutual dependency between form and content pertains as well to Ivan's telling of "The Grand Inquisitor," in which the dramatic details are continually interrupted by Alesha, who requests clarification and immediate explanation of their meaning. The nature of this structural bond is again defined by the dynamic interaction between narrative form ("The Grand Inquisitor") and the direct exposition of an idea (Ivan's responses to Alesha's questions) left momen-

tarily uncouched in drama. Such is the format, then, of both
chapters, "Rebellion" and "The Grand Inquisitor," which
together form the nucleus of Ivan's dialectic. Further, by virtue
of their being made from this bond, typical of the novel as a
whole, their structures mirror the novel's own overall structure
or underlying conception. For the novel's structure is dependent upon the union of concept and form within the main plot,
on the primary plane, and—as the main focus of our discussion—
on the bond between the same ideas and related subtexts on the
novel's secondary plane. To the extent, moreover, that one
group of subtexts enters into syntagmatic relations (for example, Ivan's collection of tales in Book Five), the result is the
emergence of a central thesis in aesthetic, narrative form; while
to the degree that a second group enters into paradigmatic
relations with the first (Zosima's string of anecdotes in Book
Six), there results an opposition between ideas, which characterizes the structure of *The Brothers* as a whole.

The ideational opposition between Books Five ("Pro and
Contra") and Six ("The Russian Monk") is clearly defined. But
within each of these books, subdivided into chapters, there are
further subdivisions into an entire series of oppositions and
contrasts, essentially among the work's subtexts, but not exclusively. In considering that latter qualification first, it is
evident that if Ivan had been given to retain only the relatively
simplistic position of blanket rejection, with no positive correlative, the stature of his argument would have been considerably
diminished, since he would have been subject to the obvious
rejoinder demanding an alternative proposition. However, his
view is only fully and completely expressed within the framework of the two adjacent chapters, which together form a single
ideational structure embracing Ivan's philosophical position.
Their juxtaposition, moreover, models the contrapuntal structure of the novel as a whole: negation ("Rebellion") is followed
by the affirmation of a new design ("The Grand Inquisitor").
Within the latter, a counter plan is evolved through a projected

travesty of Biblical parable. From so unexpected a source, the power-wielding formula, "miracle, mystery, and authority," is generated as the philosophical base for a new order founded on slavery rather than free will. In the Grand Inquisitor's ingenious dialectic lies the challenge—extending far beyond simple negation of "rebellion"—to a complacent acceptance of what Ivan considers to be an unjust order. Thus the two linked chapters contain the challenging dualistic development of Ivan's nihilistic view, and incorporate both the rationale behind his rebellion and the counter plan for a new order offered by his own fictional ideational counterpart.

In reviewing the juxtaposition of subtexts in the central part of the novel, let us begin with the chapter on the Grand Inquisitor. Ivan launches his argument with what he terms his "literary preface," in which he summarizes the apocryphal work, "The Wanderings of Our Lady through Hell," telling of the Virgin's descent and subsequent efforts to help the tormented. Ivan concludes his brief account of the ancient tale by quoting its traditional praise of God's work: "Thou art just, O Lord . . . " He explains as well that his own literary effort would have been on that order if it had been composed in an earlier period: "Well, my poem would have been of that kind if it had appeared at that time" (228). Thus he considers the work from the heritage of old Russian literature as anachronistic and antithetical to the modern temper, and the spirit of his own (the setting notwithstanding) as compatible with contemporary thinking. His reference to the medieval tale serves a distinct purpose: he means for his own effort, in which God is taken to task, to be viewed as a contrastive work—and, in another sense, as parallel to his "poem," since the Virgin, too, launches her own limited "mutiny."[6] Juxtaposed to the naive religious tale, Ivan's allegory is meant to be representative of a more sophisticated modern age. Within the single chapter, then, there is again evident a distinct contrapuntal plan. Ultimately encompassing the novel in its entirety, that plan extends to the dualistic development of Ivan's position, articulated within the two consecutive chapters at hand, and further, to the juxtaposition of the two books that express the novel's two opposing views.

Contrasted to the figure of the imperious Grand Inquisitor is that of the ideal Russian monk. Zosima's portrait is composed of isolated events in his life followed by a direct exposition of the resultant ideas and teachings which evolved from that life. Book Six follows the pattern of the traditional saint's life by relating a number of episodes from a life virtuously lived, beginning with childhood and concluding with the edifying manner in which death is met. As an inserted genre, it represents an interlude in the overall composition of the novel. Within a simple contiguous framework of several separate stories, it also details the highlights of Zosima's early years before entering the monastery. In contrast to Ivan's narration of "The Grand Inquisitor," during which there are interruptions leading to dialogue, but where the work is told rather than dramatized in story form, the biographical notes, as device, are intentionally reduced throughout to a "purely" diegetic narrative mode. In effect, the novelist "bares the device" by acknowledging in the preface to the "Notes" that concision, brevity, and the story form, unadulterated by dialogic discourse, are essential for conveying material which may be deemed irrelevant to the main action of the novel, but which is crucial to its ideational plan.

Paralleling Ivan's critical evocation of "The Virgin's Descent," in which God's plan is praised, Zosima cites the story of Job. But in contradistinction to Ivan's cursory reference to the ancient apocryphal tale which he considers to be an anachronism, Zosima sees the Biblical tale in general, and that of Job in particular, as being highly relevant to the existential dilemmas confronting modern man. In contemplating the Scriptures, he remarks: "What a miracle, what strength is given with it to man. . . . And what mysteries are solved and revealed . . . " Like the Grand Inquisitor, Zosima recognizes and is awed by the power of miracle and mystery. But these are viewed by him as spiritual values, rather than as the raw ideological material from which a political power base may be evolved. For Zosima, the ultimate resolution of miracle and mystery is not within the realm of the powers given to man. ("The greatness of [the story of Job] lies just in the fact that it is a mystery—that the passing earthly show and the eternal verity are brought together in it." 271). Authority is thus a feature of God's domain. While Zosima speaks of spiritual wealth, the Grand Inquisitor concentrates upon social and political control. The one is concerned with freedom; the other, with slavery. This is the major contrast, of course, and is therefore developed—not only on the novel's primary plane but also on the secondary—through such striking juxtapositions as Ivan's disenchanted citation of "The Virgin's Descent" countered by Zosima's enraptured account of the story of Job.

In addition to the evident compositional parallel between Ivan's and Zosima's respective evocations of the ancient tales—each from a diametrically opposed point of view—a thematic parallel may also be observed between "The Grand Inquisitor" itself and the story of Job, since in both stories God and the Devil act as opposing forces, with a human figure obliged to choose between them. While Ivan's character acknowledges that he has chosen to be in league with the Devil that his ends might be accomplished, Job, in contrast, retains his faith. Thus, in this respect as well, each story is representative of its individual proponent.

The first of Zosima's stories ("Father Zosima's Brother") tells of the spiritual regeneration which an older brother experiences, and which enables him to accept his impending early death with grace and dignity. His conversion occurs as the result of a simple revelation concisely formulated: "everyone is responsible to all men for all men and for everything" (268). The problem of achieving the "eternal harmony" that troubles

Ivan is, for him, immediately resolved by allowing oneself to perceive what is in his, and later Zosima's, view given to all men to perceive: that all creatures live and die according to a single plan, and that their lives are intertwined as part of this order. Markel's revelation and his quiet acceptance of death are the central motifs of this first story, concerned with his formative influence and the lasting impression made on Zosima.

The theme of spiritual regeneration is further developed in later parts of the biography ("Recollections of Father Zosima's Youth Before He Became a Monk. The Duel," "The Mysterious Visitor"), which are also stories of conversion, the one focusing on Zosima and his recognition of a higher plan than that of master and man, the other, on a murderer who repents of his crime. The ideational thread running through each of the stories, as the leitmotif of moral responsibility, is Markel's liberating revelation. The stories depict the idea's transmission—from Markel to Zosima, and from the latter to the murderer—becoming a motivating intellectual and moral force in their lives. By recognizing and accepting responsibility for his actions, the protagonist of each story becomes converted to the notion that "each is responsible before everyone for everyone and everything"—which he then transmits to some other sufferer and potential spiritual convert. In accordance with such chain of possible conversion, it is precisely this problem that Ivan must wrestle with at the novel's close. Developed initially within the book's secondary plane of narrative, as a series of personal anecdotes related to Zosima, the same issue finds its culmination within the main plot as Ivan's overwhelming paramount concern.

The novel's opposing ideas, underlying its basic conception, are thus developed in significant measure by narrative forms that are manifested within its secondary plane. But this only partially accounts for the complex interaction between idea and drama (form and concept), which is realized in far greater measure as the primary plane of narrative. Corresponding to

the novel's governing opposition, in which a Christian viewpoint is confronted by a fundamentally atheistic view, are the
two principal ideas succinctly formulated in nuclear ideological
form as "everything is permitted" and "everyone is responsible
for all and everything to everyone." On the primary plane, the
former finds its dramatic enactment and eventual collapse in
the series of events beginning with the murder of Fedor Pavlovich, and concluding with Smerdyakov's subsequent suicide,
followed by Ivan's breakdown. The latter teaching finds its
dramatic realization in such scenes as Alesha and Grushenka's
exchange of "onions," Dmitry's dream of the "babe" initiating
his newly found "hymn," Zosima's meeting with the peasant
women, and the gathering of the children around Alesha at the
stone. Paralleling these positive developments of the idea,
promoting love through recognizing one's responsibility for
others, there are, moreover, dramatic realizations acknowledging a corresponding negative aspect: Dmitry is ultimately
held responsible for the murder of his father; Alesha is unfairly
made accountable for his brother's assault on Captain Snegirev;
Ivan feels that he is made to pay for the insult suffered by
Katerina Ivanovna from Dmitry. Both Ivan's and Zosima's views
are thus developed, first, as the primary plot, centering on the
murder of Fedor Pavlovich, and, second, as a series of subtexts
integrated into the work to lend substance and credence to its
principal ideas.

In virtually all instances, the ideational stratum of the novel
underlies and informs the dramatic. The atheistic idea
sanctioning free will in the absence of any moral compunction
is developed, therefore, within the main action of the novel in
the murder of Fedor Pavlovich and the ultimate capitulation of
the perpetrators. Ivan's challenge to the moral order is
elaborated in "Rebellion," with its collection of cruel tales, and
given further dramatic form in the consequent revision of
society proposed and documented in "The Grand Inquisitor."
Zosima's contrastive conception of there being an underlying

unity or governing plan in the universe is dramatized in the chain of closely linked stories in which the recognition of a transcendental claim on the individual is the repeated theme buttressed by Zosima's Biblical allusions. But in support of these ideas, the sources are diametrically opposed: Ivan cites the newspapers and history books; Zosima, the Bible. On this important level, then, the literal is again confronted by the symbolic. However, in both cases, the structural pattern remains the same: the idea is confirmed and supported by the story form into which it is integrated. Narrative form and concept are bound in a single unit, defining, in effect, the novel as ideational construct.

The concluding part of Book Six, however, composed of Zosima's teachings, represents a critical exception. There an overriding concept is bereft of narrative form; exposition of idea is not realized in drama. Hence the inclusion of the extended rhetorical passages diverges from the overall structure of the novel since they lack integration within the greater narrative form. This part of the book stands as the exception to a poetics that specifies a structural bond, embracing (narrative) form and (philosophical) concept, on several planes, as being definitive of the work's underlying conception.

In considering the ideational contrast between Books Five and Six, a theodicy, or complete justification of the present order, is opposed by a corresponding indictment arguing against the existence of an underlying governing moral concept. This latter view is countered by Markel's recognition of an essential unity pervading the natural order, which yields the precept at the core of the Christian idea, as it is expressed in the novel and repeatedly echoed by those attaining a similar vision. The deep contrasts in thought and modes of perception conveyed in the two books extend especially to the respective views of man developed in each. The Grand Inquisitor's contemptuous vision of him as a morally weak creature is juxtaposed to Zosima's faith in his innate spiritual capacities. Complex dialectic is opposed

by a repeated emphasis on simplicity. The circuitous and difficult path to understanding is countered by a direct and immediate perception of the unity and order of the world.

The basic consideration which has led Ivan to "return his
ticket" is the conjecture that the world's suffering is unneces-
sary. In this notion is established the polarity between his view
and Zosima's, since the basic opposition between the two
centers on the problem of suffering. All of Ivan's tales portray
the needless suffering inflicted by humanity on itself; all of
Zosima's affirm the regeneration of a soul through moral torment and spiritual reflection. Ivan's accounts, imbued with an
aura of authenticity, serve to document the single-minded idea
of the ultimate rejection of "god's world," refracted through a
series of grotesque prisms. Counterbalancing these is Zosima's
personalized collection of stories in which all of the
protagonists—like Grushenka, in contrast to the old woman in
her tale—have discovered themselves links in the chain of
humanity.

Ivan and His Devil. The Idea Rejected.

As a place of suffering, an image of hell is evoked by Fedor
Pavlovich when he ruminates on the possibility of his being
dragged down by devils with hooks. A similar evocation is accomplished when Grushenka relates her tale of the old woman
in the burning lake; when Ivan makes reference to the apocryphal legend of "The Virgin's Descent"; when Liza confesses to
Alesha that she dreams of devils, and he admits to having the
same kind of dream. The novel is conditioned by the repeated
consideration that hell exists in some material or psychological form. Zosima considers that hell is the inability to love.
Dmitry's coachman believes in its material existence, while
for Fedor Pavlovich, its concrete manifestation represents only
a remote possibility. The latter wishes that it might have a

ceiling, but acknowledges that it probably does not, thus providing a hint that certain aspects of hell may well surface into the world of the Karamazovs. And, indeed, this is what happens, when Father Ferapont sees devils poking out of pockets and from behind doors, or when Dmitry's state of hellish torment is reflected in the chaotic scene which he instigates and fuels at the tavern in Mokroe. The raucous state of affairs of that external setting mirrors Dmitry's disoriented internal state, just as the appearance of Ivan's devil reflects the internal disintegration of the young thinker, who of himself gives rise to his shabby, unwelcome visitor—the manifestation of an idea gone bankrupt.

The conception of hell in the novel is that of an unfixed place with no real boundaries. It is that which is borne internally by some characters, while conceived of materially by others. The devil's domain extends into outer space, as he himself explains, and yet differs very little from that of the Karamazovs', in degree, evidently, more than in kind ("We have everything you have ... " 610). In any case, hell remains essentially fluid—a force that is undefined and uncontained, and very much present in the world of the Karamazovs, as something with which Ivan, more than any other character, must deal.

When Ivan arrives home, after his third and last meeting with Smerdyakov, he is in a state of momentary exhilaration (having just looked after the peasant whom he had earlier left to freeze in the snow). That feeling is immediately succeeded by extreme depression (since he has postponed his confession to the authorities until the following day, indicative, as he well knows, of an unheroic vacillation that ultimately leaves Dmitry unvindicated). At the final meeting between master and man, brother and brother, Ivan recognizes that an insect has crept into that imagined select elite for whom all is lawful. Gazing upon his lackey, Ivan sees himself, and thus is evoked his nightmare: seeing himself, he sees his devil and, in the course of this final "encounter," his ideology (thrown up at him by this same "poor relation") for what it is. After the final meeting between ideologist and instrument, it is only left for Ivan's petty devil to make his appearance in the warped psychical mirror of the once proud author of "The Grand Inquisitor." Thus the tension within him quickly finds its focus of concentration: "At last his eyes were fastened intently on one point. . . . he looked sideways at the same point . . . There was evidently something, some object, that irritated him there, worried him and tormented him" (601).

The despised object of his attention turns out to be dressed in outdated uncoordinated attire, peculiarly matched only to the motley discourse soon to follow. The method by which Ivan's devil goes about his work is to mix serious considerations with banal anecdotes, thereby effecting a sorry conglomeration, which its original author can only find abhorrent, but must now confront, filtered through the pathetic manifestation of his own disoriented state. First reflected in the brilliant light of "The Grand Inquisitor," Ivan's speculations are now reduced to cheap mental gymnastics, gross banalities mouthed by a paltry ideological lackey.

Ivan suggests at one point that, if his visitor indeed wishes to be diverting, as he claims, he recite an anecdote. The devil responds with what he emphasizes three times as being a "legend," a piece shortly to emerge as one of Ivan's earlier literary efforts, but which is already linked by this emphasis to his later, more sophisticated dialectic, "The Legend of the Grand Inquisitor." In relating the earlier piece, the devil tells of a philosopher sentenced for his lack of faith to walk a quadrillion kilometers in ether before the gates of heaven will be opened to him. He balks for a thousand years, then gets up and walks the assigned distance. When the gates are finally opened, he exclaims that for these two seconds one might walk a quadrillion quadrillion—at which point Ivan interrupts: "I've caught you! . . . That anecdote about the quadrillion years, I made up myself!" (611). Thus, by means of the anecdote, resurrected from the past, the identity of the devil as Ivan's alter ego is crystallized—paralleling previous instances ("An Onion", "The Controversy", Kolya's marketplace adventure) when the subtext has also served to identify or clarify relations among the novel's principal characters.

Yet the devil as character represents a complex problem. In him two intentions interlace: the devil is at the same time noncorporeal, the nightmarish emanation of a bankrupt intellect, but is also depicted as a character in his own right with specific characteristic motivations. On the one hand, he functions as a device to reveal further the strained nature of Ivan's internal philosophical debate; on the other, like any other character in the novel, he is subject to those governances by which his own particular nature is determined, making him an independent psychological construct during the course of his verbal encounter with Ivan.

In order to encompass fully his dualistic characterization, the devil must be abhorrent to Ivan, so that Ivan will appear repellent to himself. In this thankless role, the devil therefore continues his troublesome monologue by relating an absurd story about a lost nose, followed by an equally pointless account of a Jesuit priest, who confesses a girl whom he then seduces. Just as Ivan had earlier utilized the story form (subtext) as a kind of ideological weapon in an abortive attempt to "convert" his brother Alesha, the device is now turned inwardly upon him—by a certain incontrovertible logic—in parodic form. For the devil's trite, innocuous tales bear directly on Ivan's conception of his own intellectual stature, which they of course diminish. Hence the anecdote functions as the device by which Ivan is now forced to confront his own creation—this banal figure abounding in cheap stories intermeshed with facile philosophical constructs—and thereby, confront himself. ("No, I was never such a flunkey! How then could my soul beget a flunkey like you?" 615).

That rhetorical question finds its curious analogue in *Crime and Punishment*. In trying to explain (one last time) what had contributed to his extraordinary decision, Raskolnikov exclaims to Sonya: "I know myself that it was the devil dragging me along. . . . the devil was pulling me along then, and . . . he made it clear to me . . . that I had not the right to travel by that road . . . He mocked me. . . !" (401-02). Whether these words may be taken as literal or figurative in the mind of Raskolnikov remains unclear. In *The Brothers*, however, the devil is both "real" in the sense that he is given speech and a physical manifestation described in some detail, but is also a figment of Ivan's disturbed imagination capable of vanishing into ether upon the proper provocation. Yet rather than appear as only a fleeting detail, Ivan's confrontation with his devil, by contrast, is dramatized as part of the main plot. Hence what is only implicit and hinted at in the earlier novel is fully developed as drama in the later work. Curiously, that drama is succinctly encapsulated in Raskolnikov's plaint ("He mocked me . . . !"), but is now clearly inaugurated in the devil's own speech ("No . . . I will speak. I came to treat myself to that pleasure" 615).

In talking with Sonya, Raskolnikov ultimately rejects his own theory; the devil accommodates Ivan in doing the same thing. The protagonist himself, in the one case, and the character's alter ego, in the other, perform the identical function in devaluing a previously upheld idea. The manner in which this is accomplished is analogous but not the same. Raskolnikov, on the one hand, is expressly shown in conflict with himself—the present "ego" with his past self. In the ensuing core dispute, which holds the central place in the formally structured dialogue between Sonya and Raskolnikov, the latter's present self vanquishes his anachronistic opponent through exteriorized verbal discourse, in which Sonya acts as intermediary in the hitherto internal dialogue between Raskolnikov's two selves now made overt. Having been confronted by Sonya,

Raskolnikov is obliged—in like dialogic manner—to confront himself.

In the case of Ivan, there is a similar confrontation between past and present selves, but no such exteriorized dispute is depicted. In this instance, where the devil explicitly challenges Ivan, no broadly encompassing framework for dialogue (as that between Sonya and Raskolnikov) exists—except as an artificial construct. Although the devil as character in his own right is distanced from Ivan through the novelist's art as some *other*, thus affording the potential for dialogue—that potential is never realized. For in quoting Ivan for most of his speech, the devil brooks no interference (or dialogue), just as Ivan's own original formulations presumably did not. What dialogue exists is interiorized within the devil's speech itself, as will be shown, rather than exteriorized, as in the earlier work.

In this duel being waged by a split personality, the devil takes advantage of the fact that Ivan is visibly succumbing to self-loathing by radically changing his tactics. The patronizing mask of well-intentioned humility is discarded; all semblance of cordiality disappears as one fragment of Ivan's psyche challenges the other. Referring first, in derisive, ironic tones, to "The Grand Inquisitor"—a tack in which its author forbids his degenerative self to continue—the devil turns to an earlier composition. "And 'The Geological Cataclysm.' Do you remember? That was a poem, now!" (615).

In initiating the final drama, the devil's challenge serves to preface a second, more detailed account of Ivan's theory than first offered by Miusov in the cell. As in the latter case, it is once again recounted in anecdotal form, but is now related from an even stronger antipathetic point of view than previously, emanating this time from Ivan himself. Irony, previously Ivan's principal rhetorical weapon, is now derisively employed against him, in one of the great subtle reversals of the novel, by an alter ego, whose recapitulation of Ivan's "Geological Cataclysm" represents a single ironic shaft directed at its original author. As the final foreclosure on a bankrupt idea, the devil's "method" is an extension of that employed during Miusov's less devastating account, where an ironic presentation accompanied by a clearly unsympathetic intonation produces a second conflicting intention interlaced with the original. The result is a speech act embroiled in internal dialogue, in which the original intent (of the author of the idea) and contradictory aim (of the speaker) are clearly opposed. As the novel's quintessential example of such discourse, the devil's principal speech is here cited of necessity in its entirety.

> "Oh, I love the dreams of my ardent young friends, quivering with eagerness for life! 'There are new men,' you decided last spring, when you were meaning to come here, 'they propose to destroy everything and begin with cannibalism. Stupid fellows! they didn't ask my advice! I maintain that nothing need be destroyed, that we only need to destroy the idea of God in man, that's how we have to set to work. It's that, that we must begin with. Oh, blind race of men who have no understanding! As soon as men have all of them denied God—and I believe that period, analogous with geological periods will come to pass—the old conception of the universe will fall of itself without cannibalism and what's more the old morality, and then everything will begin anew. Men will unite to take from life all it can give, but only for joy and happiness in the present world. Man will be lifted up with a spirit of divine Titanic pride and the man-god will appear. From hour to hour extending his conquest of nature infinitely by his will and his science, man will feel such lofty joy from hour to hour in doing it that it will make up for all his old dreams of the joy of heaven. Everyone will know that he is mortal and will accept death proudly and serenely like a God. His pride will teach him that it's useless for him to repine at life's being a moment, and he will love his brother without need of reward.

> Love will be sufficient only for a moment of life, but
> the very consciousness of its momentariness will inten-
> sify its fire, which now is dissipated in dreams of
> eternal love beyond the grave' . . . and so on and so on
> in the same style. Charming!"

Ivan can only sit holding his hands to his ears looking down at
the floor, as the voice continues.

> "The question now is, my young thinker reflected, is it
> possible that such a period will ever come? If it does,
> everything is determined and humanity is settled for-
> ever. But as, owing to man's inveterate stupidity, this
> cannot come about for at least a thousand years, every-
> one who recognizes the truth even now may legitimate-
> ly order his life as he pleases, on the new principles. In
> that sense, 'all things are lawful' for him. What's more,
> even if this period never comes to pass, since there is
> no God and no immortality anyway, the new man will
> become the man-god, even if he is the only one in the
> whole world, and promoted to his new position, he may
> lightheartedly overstep all the barriers of the old mor-
> ality of the old slave-man, if necessary. There is no law
> for God. Where God stands the place is holy. Where I
> stand will be the foremost place . . . 'everything is per-
> mitted' and that's the end of it! That's all very charm-
> ing, but if you want to swindle why do you want a moral
> sanction for doing it? But that's our modern Russian
> all over. He can't bring himself to swindle without
> a moral sanction. He is so in love with truth . . ."
> (615-16)

The devil initiates his talk with an openly derisive tone
("Oh, I love dreams"), heightened by a condescending mode of
address ("'There are new men,' you decided; my young thinker
reflected"). Ivan's superior pronouncements make him a vul-
nerable target, as his pompous epithets and pronouncements

are flung back at him ("Stupid fellows; blind race of men; owing
to man's inveterate stupidity")—concluding with the gross parallelism: "Where God stands . . . /Where I stand . . . " These
verbal constructs belong, of course, to Ivan himself as reported
speech; however, the contrastive intonations by which they are
now expressed are, indeed, the devil's own work, as are a number of crude assessments punctuating his speech ("and so on
and so on; charming; and that's the end of it; that's all very
charming"). There is thus a clear verbal inlay composed of the
devil's words incorporated within the greater framework of
those expressly attributed to Ivan, and this superimposition of
one speech act upon another creates an internal dialogue within
a verbal structure that might otherwise appear as monologue.
Again, "almost every word in the narrative . . . figures simultaneously in two intersecting contexts, two speech acts: in the
speech of the author-narrator (ironic and mocking) and the
speech of the hero (who is far removed from this irony)"
(Voloshinov 1973:136). In this abstract formulation the case of
Ivan and his contemptuous alter ego is thus aptly contained.

As in Miusov's earlier report, Ivan's youthful penchant for
uncompromising formulations is again highlighted, but this
time through an entire series of hyperbolic pronouncements,
representing both the very substance of the speech itself and
its most condemning aspect:

> destroy everything; begin with cannibalism; nothing
> need be destroyed; we only need to destroy; that
> period . . . will come to pass; the old conception of the
> universe will fall; everything will begin anew; men will
> unite; man will be lifted up; man will feel; everyone
> will know . . . and will accept; everything is determined;
> humanity is settled forever; everyone . . . now may . . .
> order his life . . . on the new principles; "all things are
> lawful"; the new man may well become . . . ; "every-
> thing is permitted" and that's the end of it! [*i shabash!*]

Clearly, the unyielding, programmatic intention is Ivan's, while the ironic intonation serving to denigrate that intention is the devil's. In effect, the grandiose formulations attributed to Ivan are immediately undermined by their negative presentation. Thus, "The devil introduces into Ivan's internal dialogue accents of mockery and hopeless condemnation . . . The devil speaks as Ivan and at the same time as 'the other person,' hostilely exaggerating and distorting his accents" (Bakhtin 1984:256). The reader is thus provided with both the sense of an uncompromising youth taking up the task of once and for all drawing up a blueprint for the future of mankind—and with its simultaneous disapproval by the speaker's taking account of that predictive effort. In that taking (or settling the) account, the devil's portrayal is characterized by two competing speech elements—Ivan's and the devil's—superimposed one upon the other, with the latter's ironic intonation debasing the ideational content of the former. The duality within Ivan is thus manifested in the structure of the discourse itself, as the verbal representation of a soul about to split while struggling to remain whole.

With the deft skill borne of (ostensible) vindictiveness, the devil weaves a tight net made from his opponent's own meditations, formulated in almost equal parts of direct and reported discourse, in whose web the latter is caught, betrayed by his own idea, and finally reduced to an ineffectual plagiarist throwing inkwells at shadows. The irony of the devil's message derives from Ivan's own words turned back upon him with the added thrust of a mocking, derisive intonation. Clearly evident in the devil's discourse, the internal polemic—the word turned back upon itself—is its basic organizational dynamic. In that verbal mesh purporting to communicate an idea, irony, in conflict with the speech's idea content, emerges as the triumphant element.

Aimed at the quintessential formula, "everything is lawful," it convincingly dismisses the concept as entirely shallow, since the devil, like Smerdyakov, conceives of the idea as something petty and far removed from the grandeur of a humanistic ideal. For the devil, it amounts to nothing more than a rationale to "swindle"; for Smerdyakov, it signals the opportunity to hit a lecherous old man on the back of the head with a paperweight, swipe a paltry three thousand, and count on the gratitude of the middle brother when the older is framed for the murder and done out of his share of the inheritance. Both of Ivan's lower selves, then, in theory (the devil) and in practice (Smerdyakov), interpret the idea for what it is—the dispensation a prideful intellectual allows himself for willful self-assertion concealed behind the veil of a false all-embracing love for mankind. Within the novel's complex dialectic, it is for the lackey to smear the veil with blood, and for the devil to strip it away—leaving Ivan to confront the concrete result of his now unadorned ideology.

Registered in a minor key, the same such conflicting speech elements are evident during Miusov's earlier derisive speech in the cell. The two instances thus form an inclusive pattern in which the idea is both expounded and at the same time rejected by means of the tension borne by what Bakhtin terms the "parodistic word," an utterance which communicates information while at the same time disputing that information. In both cases, essentially the same argument is filtered through an unsympathetic voice, whose ironic tone is intended to defeat the idea, which is at the same time both communicated and deprecated. It is through Miusov that the central idea, "everything is lawful," gets its first airing. It is left to Ivan's devil finally to snuff it out.

*

Within the limited framework of this chapter, only some of the novel's subtexts have been discussed with the aim to show the semantic cohesion that arises from their variously considered juxtapositions. Delimited at the outset by a model aimed at isolating distinct narrative units from within the greater text, the novel's subtexts are conceived as individual synchronic units situated within the novel's otherwise unbroken continuum. Located outside its temporal and (frequently) spatial boundaries, the subtext is set apart from the greater story told by the novelist. That such instances of past oriented accounts deserve attention is confirmed by their interrupting the "present" narrative to make specific comment upon it. In doing so, the subtext functions as an internal modeling system, mirroring the novel's governing ideational concerns and plot intrigues through oblique or parodic reference. Our intent has thus been to map out the novel in terms of its principal iconic signs, designed to support or refute its main philosophical ideas. Occupying various positions of contrast or equivalence along the syntagmatic-paradigmatic axes, and accommodating thereby various ideational oppositions, the subtext generates meaning complementary to that of the primary text.

In brief overview, the anecdotes centering on Smerdyakov distinguish him from Ivan, while the incorporated tale ("The Controversy") foreshadows their later fatal partnership. In similar fashion, Miusov's anecdotes directed at Ivan project the internalized division between atheist and believer, culminating in the devil's startling appearance—again signifying a tortured, split psyche. Grushenka's childhood tale reflects negatively Zosima's precept that the individual is responsible to the entire human collective of which he is a part; the stories of his own life, in turn, present the idea positively. This is also the case within the main plot (primary plane) of the novel, where Zosima's idea finds its extensive development and dramatization in Ivan's decision to accept moral responsibility for the crime, and in Dmitry's parallel conclusion reached after his dream of the child. Dmitry's dream and his subsequent understanding of his own role in the child's suffering provide the answer to Ivan's tales of suffering children—which are again countered by Zosima's stories arguing the opposing point of view: that when man acknowledges his responsibility for others, through recognition of the moral order pervading the universe, his and others' suffering will cease. From Ivan's recalcitrant perspective, illustrated by his arsenal of tales, man not only does not accept responsibility for his acts (of cruelty), but prefers to forgo both his freedom and his accountability ("The Grand Inquisitor").

On still another, lesser axis of opposition, Ivan's major literary effort is paralleled by the tale of "The Virgin's Descent"—and further contrasted by Zosima's recollection of the tale of Job. Ivan's entire position is parodied, moreover, by Kolya's tale of his adventures in the marketplace, itself a minor grotesque, and secondary-level narration, but realized in full dramatic form on the primary, as murder. Other subtexts likewise have their analogues on the novel's primary plane: Zosima's story of the repentant murderer resembles Ivan's spiritual sojourn in its basic motifs, while Zosima's chronicle of his early military career parallels Dmitry's. Finally, Ivan's entire theoretical position is challenged and undermined by the devil's own collection of tales borrowed from the novel's fated theoretician and utilized against him. Thus, within this limited series, the high degree of integration between subtext and primary plot, between secondary and primary levels of narrative, and the philosophical views underlying them, becomes an evident feature of the novel's structure, whose governing ideational plan might well be elaborated from just the "secondary" perspective, which has characterized the present point of view.

In the last analysis, the aim here has been to show that the novel's structure may be legitimately viewed as a mosaic of small story forms or subtexts, which unify—and are themselves unified within—the one greater text, itself conceived as an extensive series of contrasts and parallels, oppositions and equivalences, given dramatic realization on both the primary and secondary levels. The main story which the novel purports to tell is thus viewed as a continuum projected in time and space, repeatedly interrupted by other stories incorporated into that continuum, affording the work balance and substance, as both narrative and ideational construct, in which the latter aspect represents the primary structural principle of the former—which is to say, of the novel as a whole.

6

Generating a Text

The Brothers Karamazov

During his frenzied trip to Mokroe ("I Am Coming, Too!"), Dmitry is in a turbulent state of mind filled with fears, doubts, and suicide plans. Suddenly he asks his coachman: "Andrey, simple soul, tell me, will Dmitry Fedorovich Karamazov go to hell, or not, what do you think?" Unable to apprehend the psychological torment which had inspired the seemingly frivolous question, the peasant responds in indirect but expansive fashion.

> I don't know, dear man, it depends on you, for you are . . . you see, sir, when the Son of God was nailed on the Cross and died, He went straight down to hell from the Cross, and set free all sinners that were in agony. And the devil groaned, because he thought that he would get no more sinners in hell. And God said to him, then, "Don't groan, for you shall have all the mighty of the earth, the rulers, the chief judges, and the rich men, and shall be filled up as you have been in all ages til I come again." Those were his very words . . . (389)

Yet the naive tale affords Dmitry a moment of respite. It also serves to document for the reader the broad gulf that separates the complex psychological motivations of the nobility from the simple peasant mentality, which, exemplified by the coachman,

sees the entire upper stratum of society condemned as a class
to a final, inescapable punishment.

The question posed by Dmitry is simply indicative of his
agitated state; the response elicited, however, goes a long way
towards explaining why he himself will be found guilty at the
trial. Although the connection between this miniature tale
representing only a minor pause in the narrative and the trial
scenes at the end of the novel may appear tenuous, the kind of
thinking expressed in the legend nevertheless reflects the
attitude of those who are to sit in judgment of Dmitry. In spite
of the virtuoso performance by the defense, the peasant will
remain firm in his views, his fixed conception of things not to
be infiltrated by intricate argumentation; for him, the realm of
psychology is more abstract and less tangible than that of the
apocrypha. The little vignette related by the coachman thus
shows how the peasants' conceptions originate—eventually har-
dening into conviction—and anticipates, in oblique fashion to
be sure, the outcome of the trial.

This small narrative encapsulates a notion of justice for the
gentry subscribed to by the coachman. By extension, it also
prefigures the final verdict pronounced by a jury of *his* (rather
than Dmitry's) peers. From a semiotic standpoint, the tale may
be regarded as an indexical sign, pointing from a secondary level
of the text (where it appears as an engaging "aside" from an
unexpected quarter) to the primary plane of action, where the
main plot unfolds and the novel's principal ideas are expounded. To regard the coachman's story from this perspective
is of present concern. For what figures as index in one episode
has the potential to generate more story in another. An account
may serve merely to prefigure later events; however, it may also
provide the rationale for, or make inevitable, the further action
of the plot. Information which serves to prefigure what is to
come offers, in effect, hints to the reader, making for greater
anticipation. When considered later, such hints afford a sense
of destiny having taken its course. The passage cited provides

just that veiled sense. By contrast, to consider that a certain account has served to generate further story is to acknowledge a relation of cause and effect, whereby a single episode clearly determines the next.

To show in some measure where the "causes" lie and where the "effects" are achieved in *The Brothers* is the aim of the present chapter. That intent depends upon demonstrating that much of the extensive narrative of the work is generated from two interrelated, complementary structures. By isolating and tracing the various transformations by which a specific motif emerges as a major theme, we may demonstrate, first, how certain crucial information issues initially from a single, limited narrative form eventually to embrace whole extended passages of the text; and, second, how these two related structural entities—the "anecdote" and "reconstruction"—function to link past and future events to a common present, while relating the story of the novel in the process. From this perspective, the task of the critic amounts to "displaying the work as a spatial configuration in which time past and time future point to one end, which is always present" (Culler 1975:244). That task, in effect, specifies our present endeavor.

In his seminal Formalist work, *Theory of Literature*, Boris Tomashevsky defines the motif as being an irreducible unit present in every sentence of a literary work. From the aggregate of motifs emerge the various themes. However, to undertake in practice a structural analysis of the literary work, the critic may first be obliged to isolate and then designate a workable complex of motifs, or some single structural entity, to serve as the basic narrative unit from which to proceed. For our purposes, the anecdotal form—previously viewed in its iconic role—will now serve as such (irreducible) unit in its generative mode. Conceived as a miniature account set outside the novel's temporal and spatial bounds, the anecdote purports to relate an especially pertinent incident occurring at another time and place from the story proper of the novel. As highly condensed narrative detail, composing seemingly isolated, distinct accounts, the anecdote will now be shown in several critical instances to progress as a well-developed leitmotif through a series of transformations, yielding major episodes and large portions of plot. In semiotic terms, it will be seen to function as indexical sign and nuclear narrative form serving to generate the novel's major themes.

In contrast to the motif, a work's most basic plot element, its theme, understood in Tomashevsky's sense as an aggregate of motifs, is manifested as drama and developed in novelistic time. Each theme necessarily unfolds within a certain spatial and temporal framework. A major premise of this discussion, however, will be that in *The Brothers*, time is not linear; what is past is not necessarily done with. An event is frequently resurrected in narrative and retold from a new perspective, providing an added or different dimension. Its significance and meaning are thus in some degree dependent upon—and born from—its "recurrence" or repeated telling. Rarely are the episodes of the novel presented as part of a causal sequential chain chronologically ordered. Rather, the novel's principal events are repeatedly discussed and recounted in various contexts where they acquire new and deeper meanings. A past episode is revivified (much like reported speech) through renarration because of a certain incumbent "present" significance which necessitates its being retold. In *The Brothers*, as will be shown, the present thus acts as a centripetal force upon the past—regenerating events by recalling them for reexamination and reinterpretation.

*

The art of story telling is Fedor Pavlovich's forte. He tells stories for his own ends and in order to provoke a reaction from others. Frequently, the result of his provocations is to inspire a counter-narration in response. And it is through these and other accounts, recapitulations, and anecdotes that the novel proceeds to tell its story and from which it is built. By fashioning some brief, abrasive, or absurd account, Fedor Pavlovich creates an atmosphere according to his liking and, generally, counter to that of all those around him. A guiding dictum of his is that an incensed opponent is bound to slip, and the more slippery the old man can make it for others, the greater the control attained for himself. In short, the story is the device by which he remakes a situation, turning his immediate environment into his own element. At the same time, it serves to make him the potential antagonist of everyone present or of whomever is willing to take up the challenge. His material is purposefully chosen and tossed off with aplomb. Details are emphasized or omitted from his accounts according to whether they are supportive or detrimental to his case. That his methods are generally effective may be gauged by the degree to which he succeeds—in virtually every scene in which he appears—in making himself the dominant figure. Nowhere do these generalizations hold truer than in the scenes set in Zosima's cell, where he narrates a whole series of absurd but provocative anecdotes by which he first attracts the company's attention and then holds it.

Almost immediately upon making his appearance, Fedor Pavlovich begins to relate outrageous stories designed to create an atmosphere of tension and strain. In clearly challenging, provocative tones, the old man repeatedly shows how easily and imperceptibly he can manage to slip into the role which titles the chapter ("The Old Buffoon"). Although intended to appear ingenuous, his conduct is not without design. Having contrived Dmitry's absence during the outset of the meeting, Fedor Pavlovich affords himself the opportunity to gauge the situation, provoke those assembled, and essentially transform the gathering into one in which he alone is comfortable and able to maneuver. His almost methodical buffoonery emanates from a simulated lack of control by which he at first unleashes an abundant flow of innocuous absurdities, followed by a series of disparaging charges and accusations directed at his son. Requiring greater consideration, the latter series represents the nuclei or kernels from which large parts of the novel emerge and take on substance as its major themes.

The situation attains its greatest negative potential, as planned by Fedor Pavlovich, only with the late appearance of the foremost incendiary element. Already stoked up from the realization of his father's crafty stratagem, Dmitry appears as the injured son bearing a grievance—which, all the same, he will never manage to articulate in efficacious manner. For in the ensuing verbal confrontation between father and son, which the former initiates with the following barrage of highly sketchy information leveled against the volatile Dmitry, Fedor Pavlovich adopts the story teller's prerogative to select and arrange material according to his personal dictates (artistic or otherwise), and thus manages to attend to his own aims with particular adroitness and to the detriment of his son, whom he has already succeeded in putting on the defensive.

> The whole town shakes and echoes with his debaucheries. And where he was stationed before, he several times spent a thousand or two for the seduction of some respectable girl; we know all about that Dmitry Fedorovich, sir, in its most secret details. I'll prove it, sir... Would you believe it, holy Father, he has captivated the heart of the most honorable of young ladies of good family and fortune, daughter of a gallant colonel, formerly, his superior officer, who had received many honors and had the Anna Order on his breast. He compromised the girl by his promise of marriage, now she is an orphan and here; she is betrothed to him, yet before her very eyes he is dancing attendance on a certain enchantress. And although

this enchantress has lived in, so to speak, civil marriage with a respectable man, yet she is of an independent character, an unapproachable fortress for everybody, just like a legal wife—for she is virtuous, yes, holy Father, she is virtuous. Dmitry Fedorovich wants to open this fortress with a golden key, and that's why he is insolent to me now, trying to get money from me, though he had wasted thousands on this enchantress already. He's continually borrowing money for the purpose. From whom do you think? Shall I say, Mitya? (62)

Interrupted by his son, Fedor Pavlovich's bombast is concluded for the moment with that final disquieting question left unanswered for nearly four hundred pages—until the preliminary investigation, when Dmitry finally reveals that he had appropriated the three thousand rubles entrusted to him by Katerina Ivanovna, in order to carry off the woman his father repeatedly refers to as an "enchantress." Ultimately having a direct bearing on the question of whether there had been a financial motive for committing the crime, the money becomes a vital detail repeatedly discussed and disputed in the novel's concluding chapters. But here first raised by Fedor Pavlovich, its significance for the reader, among a host of other details, remains completely opaque.

Directly following his first verbal offensive, only momentarily disrupted by his son, Fedor Pavlovich launches another, but on a different front.

Gentlemen, only fancy; there's a poor but honorable man living here, burdened with a numerous family, a captain who got into trouble and was discharged from the army, but not publicly, not by court-martial, with no slur on his honor. And three weeks ago, our Dmitry Fedorovich seized him by the beard in a tavern, dragged him out into the street by that very beard, and

> beat him publicly, and all because he is an agent in a
> little business of mine. (63)

Again interrupted, Fedor Pavlovich's anecdotal plaint against his son concludes on that vague note. Yet his extended discourse, in its entirety, contains the novel's principal motifs— the broken betrothal, carnal love, the rivalry between father and son for the love of the same woman (arising as a direct consequence of his words rather than as part of them), and the humiliation of a defenseless individual. From each of these motifs are generated the novel's major themes within the dramatized sequences of events related to each. The anecdotal form thus embraces the vital details, or "dynamic" motifs (to borrow Tomashevsky's usage), which are the respective sources from which the corresponding themes emerge into fully developed form.

Containing in embryo several of the complex relationships of the novel, the old man's diatribe provides the first representation of Dmitry's fractured relationship with Katerina Ivanovna, includes the first reference in the novel to Grushenka and her involvement with the old merchant Samsonov, and recounts the story of Captain Snegirev's unfortunate encounter with Fedor Pavlovich's oldest son and chief rival. As a contributing factor to the sustained quality of opacity, each of the characters is left unnamed for the present, and remains to the reader virtually unknown. In effect, all of the scant pieces of information provided are but shadows hinting at still concealed structures. But stated in their most minimal form by Fedor Pavlovich, as no more than a string of bare motifs, they are later to evolve into the large chunks of story from which the novel is made.

Fedor Pavlovich's account of Dmitry's activities is notable, on the one hand, for its lack of explanatory detail, but also, for the extravagant exaggeration by which he casts aspersions on his son. Both aspects of the account contribute to a distorted picture, which is only later revised or qualified during the course of the novel. Dmitry registers the resultant imbalance when he vociferously denies his father's bare imputations: "It's all a lie! Outwardly it's the truth, but inwardly, a lie!" (63). The complaint acknowledges, in effect, that Fedor Pavlovich has turned the anecdote into an effective instrument by which he maintains the role of antagonist, while keeping his son on the defensive. His charge that Dmitry has compromised his highly deserving betrothed in order to seduce another, thus remains— for the time being at least—unchallenged and unqualified.

The counterpoint to Fedor Pavlovich's attempted character assassination is provided later (in the three linked chapters, "The Confession of a Passionate Heart"), when the situations to which Fedor Pavlovich alludes are reformulated, again primarily in anecdotal form. But on that occasion, the bare statement of fact is now enhanced with added dimensions as Dmitry depicts the moral struggle, which had been highly relevant to the outcome of the tense encounter between military officer leading a profligate existence and proud aristocratic young woman come to barter for the sake of her father's honor: "My first idea was a—Karamazov one . . . I went to the window, put my forehead against the frozen pane, and I remember the ice burned my forehead like fire" (102-03). The psychological complexities of his relationship with Katerina Ivanovna also find expression ("She loves her own virtue, not me." 105), as does the additional complicating factor of his infatuation with Grushenka, whom he equates with the "back alley ways," where one may find "adventure, the unexpected, and precious metal in the dirt." Because Fedor Pavlovich's account is abstracted of all qualifying detail, including that of a moral or psychological nature, it operates on a purely surface level employing the barest facts, as a series of motifs, which of themselves preclude other relevant aspects. During the preliminary investigation, a parallel situation occurs when the authorities ignore the psychological-moral plane of Dmitiry's actions, to which he continually refers, and indict him on the basis of what seem to be the facts.

Fedor Pavlovich's abbreviated pronouncements in the cell, followed by Dmitry's later relatively expanded accounts, are contrastive versions representing separate, distinct stages of a narrational method employed throughout the novel: the direct exposition of facts denuded of relevant detail, consistently followed by a fuller reconstruction of the same events, incorporating such details as will allow for their association by the reader with others which have come to light. This method, in effect, provides for their fuller comprehension at a later, crucial moment, by providing added contours to an otherwise truncated or distorted account—an aspect of the general novelistic technique of simply parceling out information at the most appropriate moments. Such moments are intended to coincide with the alleviation of suspense on certain counts and with its reinforcement on others. In *The Brothers*, one method by which this is achieved is the usage of contrastive segments of narrative concerned with the same subject. Fedor Pavlovich's utterly spare account, for instance, gives rise of necessity to Dmitry's greater elaboration of the same concerns, all of which results in the obviation for the reader of certain questions, while new ones arise.

What this represents is a recurrent pattern of "allusions," by which an incident or relationship is first barely mentioned, and only later expanded upon. The pattern holds true in the case of Dmitry, who tells of his broken betrothal only after it has been referred to by his father; in the case of Grushenka, who speaks of her liaison with the Pole after he has been mentioned by Katerina Ivanovna and the narrator; and in that of Captain Snegirev, who tells of the ill treatment received at Dmitry's hands after it has been referred to by Fedor Pavlovich and Katerina Ivanovna. In each case, the situation is only remarked upon briefly, so that the reader becomes aware of its occurrence, but not of its significance.

At a later, crucial or poignant moment, the importance of the situation will become evident when it is related by the character most affected by it, and therefore slated to be the "authority" on what has transpired. Thus, Dmitry knows best why he has broken with Katerina Ivanovna (explaining to Alesha that her reforming instinct and Grushenka have come between them); Grushenka alone knows the feeling of resentment and pain harbored for five years (and then relinquished in a moment as she flies to the "first and rightful" lover); while Captain Snegirev relates most poignantly what the incident in front of the tavern meant for him and, especially, his son. Consistently employed, this narrative method allows for an episode to be filtered through a number of viewpoints, frequently as rumor or hearsay. In this manner, it undergoes various transformations—until it is expressed most vividly by that character who has suffered or experienced the event. The episode itself thus attains a certain dynamic quality, through such repeated references, within a novel that is built up in large measure out of events which are charged and recharged with new significance and meaning.

A single incident is thus frequently related from a number of perspectives, until it emerges with the greatest significance that is to be attached to it, ending when it is finally and conclusively told—essentially as a final pronouncement on the past—by a single character most in a position to know. Those events occurring during the time span covered by the novel, and therefore receiving an initial depiction on its primary plane of action (as part of the mainstream of events), accrue added significance, generally of a psychological nature, by their later reconstruction. Events which have occurred earlier than the time span of the novel (Dmitry's meeting with Katerina Ivanovna, Grushenka's liaison, Snegirev's humiliation) are related in anecdotal form. It is in such form that these episodes are projected into the main plot, becoming contiguous with it and propelling it, by eliciting further action or dialogue in the form of new episodes.

The immediate function of Fedor Pavlovich's diatribe in the cell is to initiate the furious discussion during which hints of shady dealings, allusions to private matters, and threats are made. But in terms of the novel's greater design, the entire scene is a device by which important themes, later to be elaborated upon, are first introduced and anticipated in condensed, indirect fashion. These include: Dmitry's fated relationship with Katerina Ivanovna, his passion for Grushenka, and his encounter with the captain. Each of these themes originates with Fedor Pavlovich's attempt to expose his son's exploits; each forms a separate thread in the overall plot of the novel (intertwined with the others to be sure); and each follows its own course of development.

The story told by Dmitry of the fateful encounter between Katerina Ivanovna and himself contains virtually all the elements which lead to their broken betrothal: pride, one-up-manship, her savior instinct, his dissolute ways. All that remains at the time the novel opens (their encounter, of course, occurs in the "past") is for Alesha to fulfill his brother's commission and pay the latter's "respects." The story of their fated relationship first enters the novel in anecdotal form, through Fedor Pavlovich's intimations in the cell, and then, in more developed fashion, through Dmitry's later, expanded "confession." Having its origins in the past, their story first appears in embryonic form, whose gradual organic development reflects the role it will play in the work as a whole, since the consequences of the severed relationship are felt throughout the course of "present" events. Dmitry's guilt at having taken the three thousand in order to carry off Grushenka thus colors his actions and his state of mind, paralleling Katerina Ivanovna's resultant injured pride. Culminating in her producing Dmitry's incriminating letter, the single most damaging piece of evidence at the trial, much of the strange "inexplicable" behavior and complex interaction on the part of the novel's "triangle" can be explained only by reference to that fateful encounter of another time and place. Thus his detailed rendering of the prideful jockeying for power, or sense of moral superiority, in which humility is employed as the basic vehicle, makes much of what takes place later ("The Laceration in the Drawing Room," the revelation of the document) plausible.

Only within the last pages of the novel ("For a Moment the Lie Becomes Truth"), do the complex relations between Dmitry and Katerina Ivanovna find their momentary resolution. The scene represents the only other occasion when the two are depicted together, although the tension between them forms an important thread in the latticework of the novel, as does each of the male/female partnerships. The title of the chapter signifies the instability of their ties; their good feelings for one another are fated to be overshadowed by Katerina Ivanovna's pride coupled with her determination to regenerate Dmitry, and by his equally steadfast resolve to resist her efforts. Their bonds are destined to remain slippery and elusive; only for a moment can the lie—the possibility of their establishing a lasting union between them—become truth. This final realization is delayed until the very close of the novel, since the tensions created by Dmitry and Katerina Ivanovna's involved interaction in the past are meticulously interwoven into the "present" relationships of Ivan and Katerina Ivanovna, and Dmitry and Grushenka—the strained ties of both "new" pairs, for the most part, originating from, and being largely dependent upon, those of the "original" couple. Moreover, the seemingly loose bonding of these volatile pairs makes for a special tension—hinging on the question of present loyalties being maintained as opposed to the ever-present threat of further shifting or dissolution of couples—which is crucial to both the suspense and the structure of the novel, and is therefore sustained to the end.

The relationship between Grushenka and the Pole, by contrast, represents an instance when the early dissolution of a pair leads to the relaxation of suspense in one quarter (as the position of the "first and rightful" suitor fades in importance)—only to augment it significantly in another (Dmitry's arrest).

During the meeting between Katerina Ivanovna and Grushenka ("Both Together"), the former coyly relates the salient features of the other's early career, concluding with the information that the original seducer is expected to return. In this case, the role of the anecdote (Katerina Ivanovna's telling of the crucial episode in her rival's past) is anticipatory of Grushenka's short-lived renewal of her acquaintanceship with the Pole. Much later in the novel, Grushenka herself gives an account (offering an "authoritative" version) of that episode in her past in which the Pole figures as hero and villain—and which had colored everything thereafter. She retells those events to which Katerina Ivanovna had earlier alluded, but her expanded narration of the anecdote is now pivotal in generating further plot developments. For with her telling of her own story, the account takes on new dimensions, as she incorporates the personal details of anguish and the desire for revenge, of which only she knows ("I'll pay him back, I'll pay him back!"). Yet at the same time, the entire episode is now updated to the present—to the very moment of decision: "Am I so abject? Shall I run to him or not?" (332). Those are the options open to her. With her maid Fenya's announcement that the expected messenger has arrived and is waiting, five year's of resentment and recrimination are disregarded as Grushenka opts for a new life—which turns out to be only a fleeting moment, an ironic footnote to the past.

In contrast to Katerina Ivanovna's initial telling of Grushenka's story, which prepares for the latter's departure and final meeting with the Pole, Grushenka's own account of her past bears on the present (and future) by the inclusion of the options open to her. Moreover, it generates the further action

of the novel by her decision to go. The earlier telling of the story
is therefore primarily indexical (or anticipatory of possible new
developments), while the latter is essentially generative, since
it leads to new episodes and more story.

Paralleling Grushenka's flight and hopes for a new life is
Dmitry's pursuit of her and similar wish, following the collapse
of the Pole as a serious rival. In short, her departure leads to
most of the events chronicled in Book Eight: Dmitry's learning
of her absence, his misguided assumption that she is with Fedor
Pavlovich, all that transpires under his father's windows, his
subsequent pursuit of her to Mokroe, and all that takes place
there. Unlike any of the other books of the novel, the one
expressly devoted to Dmitry is composed of pure action organized according to a simple causal sequential pattern, as he
runs clutching at straws in a series of vain attempts to raise
funds. There is no elaboration of ideas and no deviation from
the main plot to a secondary plane of narrative; there are no
references to past events (in the form of anecdotes) and no
devices which deflect Dmitry from his fatal course. For Dmitry
there is no respite; for the reader there is the sense of inex-
orable destiny taking its course, not unmixed with a certain
comic aspect ever bordering on pathos: Dmitry's fruitless efforts at rousing Lyagavy—a sorry figure even for a last recourse,
his conversation with Mme. Khokhlakova composed almost
entirely of non sequiturs, her untimely fixation on the gold
mines. The few rapturous moments spent with Grushenka
("Delirium") conclude with the pathetic denouement of Dmitry's arrest. And with this unexpected reversal, the course of
the novel takes a new turn, as its central event, the murder of
Fedor Pavlovich, attains to the foremost place, with much that
is left of the novel (Book Nine: "The Preliminary Investigation," the three interviews between Ivan and Smerdyakov, and
the final book devoted to the trial) directed toward unraveling
the mystery.

Once the murder is accomplished and a thing of the past, the novel shifts compositionally, at the close of Book Eight, as the prevalence of anecdotes reflecting back on the past diminishes, giving way to a new form—the reconstruction of events already depicted as part of the main action (and therefore familiar to the reader), but which receive new consideration as new values are attributed. From these recapitulations, never attaining more than partial accuracy, arise ambiguities that testify both to a certain autonomy belonging to the past and to the imperviousness of man's actions, never fully susceptible to psychological analysis.

In conformity with the novel's contrapuntal scheme, the image of the injured captain eventually appears as the counterpoint figure in the important pervasive theme of fatherhood. What takes place in the hut, occurring in an atmosphere of love, represents the counterbalance to the principal manifestation of the theme, concentrated on the loveless relationship between Fedor Pavlovich and his sons. While the relevant facts of Snegirev's situation are briefly mentioned by Fedor Pavlovich in the cell, the central motif of the poor man burdened by a large family remains undisclosed. But from this single, as yet buried detail will gradually emerge a fully delineated picture of the attendant hardships: Snegirev's personal plight, his family beleaguered by illness, and especially the wasting figure of his little son are to be drawn with pathos, attaining depth and dimension. Although there is no reference made by Fedor Pavlovich to the children, his anecdotal account of the episode in front of the tavern is indexical in pointing to a more detailed recapitulation of the incident and in preparing, in effect, for the eventual introduction of the boys into the novel. In thematic terms, his sole intent in relating the event is to denigrate his son before an audience, and thus achieve the edge he seeks. But in terms of the novel's greater plan, his sketch also allows for the entire later development of this prominent theme.

In "A Meeting with the Schoolboys," Alesha is attacked and cruelly bitten by one of them. There is no indication as to who the vindictive child might be, nor is there any explanation for the unprovoked attack (except that Alesha is a Karamazov). Yet the other boys are aware of something of which Alesha (and the reader) is not. The initial exposition of the Snegirev incident, in the form of Fedor Pavlovich's anecdote, followed by this first scene with the boys, is thus structured along parallel lines characterized by the omission of elucidative detail, yielding further unanswered questions and a modicum of suspense. Such explanatory detail is provided only later through subsequent narrations of the former incident. By undergoing transformations inherent in the addition of new information, these later accounts are to lend a clearer understanding of what had motivated the unknown boy's attack in the first place.

Shortly after Alesha's puzzling encounter with the schoolboys, but more than one hundred pages after Fedor Pavlovich's account of his son's assault on the captain, Katerina Ivanovna refers to the same event, in connection with her intent to offer financial recompense to the victim of the same man who has grossly insulted her pride. In requesting that Alesha assist her in the undertaking, she recounts the details of the incident which have prompted her to make an offer of compensation.

> A week—yes, I think it was a week ago—Dmitry Fedorovich was guilty of a hasty and unjust action—a very ugly action. There is a low tavern here and in it he met that discharged officer, that captain, whom your father used to employ in some business. Dmitry Fedorovich somehow lost his temper with this captain, seized him by the beard and dragged him out into the street and for some distance along it, in that insulting fashion. And I am told that his son, a boy, quite a child, who is at the school here, saw it and ran beside them crying and begging for his father, appealing to everyone to defend him, while everyone laughed. (176)

Told from the perspective of the proud but sensitive Katerina Ivanovna, a new factor is disclosed: the poignant detail of the son subjected to the sight of his father being publicly humiliated. From this motif (completely omitted from Fedor Pavlovich's original narration of the same incident) is generated the entire theme of the boys with their initial animosity towards and later compassionate understanding for Ilyusha and his suffering. Katerina Ivanovna's account thus brings a main element of the whole affair into focus for the first time, resolving the enigma of the schoolboy's inexplicable behavior towards Alesha, who quickly surmises the connection.

Far from being gratuitously motivated, this second narration of the same incident is integrated as a necessary preface to Katerina Ivanovna's request that Alesha offer the captain the two hundred rubles as recompense in the name of his assailant's betrothed. The anecdote retold thus has regressive relevance, since it provides a partial explanation of preceding events (Alesha's initial encounter with the boy), while at the same time it generates further related events, since Katerina Ivanovna's commission necessitates Alesha's visit to the Snegirev family. The anecdote thus functions as important linkage, or as a dual-directed sign, that may be conceived schematically as follows.

Past Event   *Future Event*

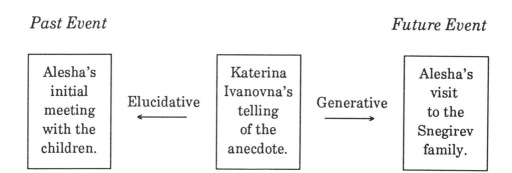

Katerina Ivanovna's recitation of the Snegirev incident is thus pivotal. While helping to explain a past episode, it also serves as a source of further developments.

Finally, the captain himself relates the story for the last time, during his meeting with Alesha, who is commissioned by Katerina Ivanovna to seek him out. Only now, in this last telling, the story emerges as the prelude to a moving account of the father's relationship with his son, whom he makes central to this most poignant and revealing account of the same incident.[1]

> And, by the way, about the boy, sir . . . I will describe that scene to you. My tow was thicker a week ago—I mean my beard, sir. That's the nickname they give to my beard, the schoolboys most of all. Well, your brother Dmitry Fedorovich was pulling me by my beard. He dragged me out of the tavern into the marketplace; at that moment the boys were coming out of school, and with them Ilyusha. As soon as he saw me in such a state, sir, he rushed up to me. "Dad," he cried, "Dad!" He caught hold of me, hugged me, tried to pull me away, crying to my assailant, "Let go, let go, it's my dad, forgive him!"—yes, he actually cried "forgive him." He clutched at that hand, that very hand, in his little hands and kissed it, sir. . . . I remember his little face at that moment. I haven't forgotten it, sir, and I never shall!" (186)

In this final account of the incident, the pathos of the schoolboy overshadows the pathetic tribulation of the father, whose humiliating experience is subordinated to his son's reaction to the scene. The subsequent narrational flow in the text is from the episode to the boy, and then to his resultant unfortunate relationship with the other children as a direct consequence of the incident. Finally, the children appear as the main focus of attention at the point when the captain makes the compelling observation: "Schoolboys are a merciless race, individually they are angels of God, but together, especially in schools, they are often merciless" (188). The remark triggers a lengthy discourse by the captain on the schoolboys and Ilyusha's unhappy role among them, thus preparing for their further, more expansive inclusion in the novel in Book Ten.

With this third telling of the story the theme of the children is imperceptibly introduced as a natural concomitant to the events described. There are virtually no seams showing; the development of the theme is so gradual, and its early generative stages so well integrated, that its very dependence on the cruel episode first related by Fedor Pavlovich for its emergence remains obscure. The stages by which this important theme gradually appears are marked by the successive narration of the same anecdote from three perspectives, each time yielding new dimensions and added poignancy. Hence there are a variety of perspectives, by which a number of viewpoints contribute to the depiction of a single event. In the present instance, each telling of the anecdote provides for the development of a theme first vaguely articulated as a parcel of unexplained dramatic action ("A Meeting with the Schoolboys"), but ultimately elaborated as an entire book of the novel ("The Children"), in which the corresponding explicit depiction of the relationships among the youthful characters—themselves the promise of a better world than that of the Karamazovs—allows for their triumphant voices at the end to sound the novel's concluding hopeful note.

*

In the first book of the novel, the reader is provided with background information to the leading figures in the drama to be unfolded. The opening chapters are a latticework of concrete detail interwoven with hints and innuendoes. What the reader learns about the traditional monastic institution of elders, for example, is direct and explicit, with several anecdotes drawn from the legendary past to underscore the mystery and awesomeness with which the institution is imbued. In contrast, what the reader learns about the family Karamazov, united after so many years, is both informative and paradoxical. Their individual histories and eventual reunion—the point at which the novel proper begins—is surrounded with an aura of ambiguity and uncertainty achieved through various techniques. The narrator, as though unwilling to rely on one source of information, credits two opposing descriptions of the same occurrence; a great number of indefinites are employed, while certain items are repeated and elaborated upon with the injunction that the particular detail be remembered; at times, the narrator simply allows that he himself is confused. In this first book, sufficient information is provided to establish events in the present; at the same time a whole series of questions are posed (beginning with the novel's opening sentence, which indicates that a catastrophe of some sort has occurred), to be answered only in the course of the subsequent narrative.

By referring back in time, the novel's first book parallels the composition of its concluding books, especially the last. While the opening book is devoted to the presentation of events which have occurred prior to the main time period encompassed by the novel, the latter books are occupied with the reconstruction or recapitulation of events which have been depicted earlier, but which require further consideration. Both poles of the novel, then, are in large measure past-oriented—but with a difference: what is described at the beginning is necessarily presented for the first time, providing the reader with the information needed to follow the story that is about to unfold; what is described at the end refers back to what has already been covered in the narrative (Smerdyakov's acount of the murder being the one exception), but with different interpretations affording new layers of significance. Events which have occurred in the distant past are thus detailed in the first book of the novel; in subsequent books, as we have seen, events which have taken place in the more recent past are related in the form of anecdotes as a source of additional needed information.

In concluding our discussion, the term "reconstruction" will be used to signify a complex system employed in the latter part of the novel, in which past events already described are given over to further consideration through new and separate accounts—a device that is typical of a work containing judicial investigations and trial scenes. The reconstruction of a past event generally utilizes an indirect mode of discourse aimed at dispensing with certain aspects of an episode in order to concentrate more closely on others. Analogous to the "partially detailed report" (Chapter Four), one aspect of an account is isolated and detailed, facilitating its greater consideration. To this end, the reconstruction is developed both in story form and dialogue, as complementary means of highlighting those specifics of particular interest. Like the anecdote, the reconstruction represents a temporal and spatial displacement by moving back in time to another setting, but with the difference that what is to be reconstructed is already familiar to the reader by virtue of its having received its initial depiction within the novel's primary plane of action. The reconstruction may thus be described as a past-oriented structure, since it, too, is concerned with what has already occurred—but which is not yet done with.

Numerous episodes receiving their initial depiction in the earlier chapters of the novel are further detailed from various perspectives in later chapters (of Books Nine, Eleven, and Twelve), where they attain new meaning by being subjected to new viewpoints. In providing additional perspectives and (contrastive) assessments of the past, the reconstruction imbues the novel's events with a multiplicity of interpretations, which highlight the ultimate complexity and ambiguity behind human behavior. Such events include virtually all of Dmitry's actions prior to his arrest (detailed in Book Eight, and reviewed in subsequent books). As the central event of the novel, the murder of Fedor Pavlovich attains the greatest amount of consideration by means of numerous reconstructions all aimed at penetrating to the meaning of the crime. The first account of what occurred "in the dark," as a case in point, is offered by Dmitry to his interlocutors during the preliminary investigation. In his initial recapitulation of those events, the emphasis falls on Dmitry's own internal struggle—as only he knows it to have been—at the moment when he might have murdered his father.

> Well it was like this. . . .Whether it was someone's tears, or my mother prayed to God, or a good angel kissed me at that instant, I don't know. But the devil was conquered. I rushed from the window and ran to the fence. My father was alarmed and, for the first time, he saw me then, cried out, and sprang from the window. I remember that very well. I ran across the garden to the fence . . . and there Grigory caught me . . . (446)

The novel's course of events is essentially interrupted by the reconstruction which casts new light on past episodes. In this respect, a certain regressive relevance may be attributed to it, since the reconstruction retards the progress of the plot in order to probe the psychological significance of what is past. In addition, it serves to generate the subsequent events of the novel. As a prominent case in point, Smerdyakov's account to his mentor of how and why the murder was committed—the novel's most fully developed examination of an event—concentrates on that event, subjecting it to an unexpectedly acute psychological analysis. In result, Smerdyakov's recapitulation of what occurred leads to his subsequent suicide, foments Ivan's sickness manifested in the appearance of his devil, and motivates Ivan's disastrous appearance in court. The reconstruction thus also functions as a dual-directed sign pointing to and elaborating upon the past, while contributing to the further development of events in the present. As a related past-oriented structure, it is analogous in this respect as well to the anecdote, which—in its generative (as opposed to purely indexical) mode—functions in like manner.

The Preliminary Investigation.

The short chapter with which Book Nine begins, "The Beginning of Perkhotin's Official Career," will serve as model. The problem of unraveling what occurred on the fatal night begins there as the story is built up—in this and succeeding chapters—from the separate facts, which each character affirms, regarding Dmitry's conduct and whereabouts during the course of that night. When Perkhotin is given to relate his account of what happened, part of what he has to say is told directly; the rest is dispensed with thus: "Briefly, but fairly clearly, Petr Ilyich told . . . the history of the affair, that part of it at least which he had himself witnessed" (423). That observation might serve as a kind of epigraph to the reconstruction as narrative technique, where only certain information is parceled out for greater consideration.

The conclusion to Book Eight (Dmitry's arrest) marks the turning point of the novel; most of the remaining chapters (with the exclusion of the entire Book Ten) are focused back in time, with virtually every character of the novel contributing an interpretation concerning some aspect of the crime. In the first chapter of Book Nine, these range from the maid Fenya's hysterical account of how Dmitry returned to her covered in blood, to Perkhotin's sober telling of how Dmitry had at first borrowed ten rubles from him and had then returned with anywhere from two to three thousand with the explanation that they had been obtained from Mme. Khokhlakova, to that venerable lady's own innocuous explanation of how Dmitry had insulted her and that she had never given him anything. In this chapter, the main plot is interlaced with reconstructions, reflecting back on Dmitry's biography, in an effort to determine his destiny. From those efforts the following pattern emerges: Perkhotin's meeting with Fenya (main plot) allows for her to render her account (reconstruction); his subsequent ruminations and decision to visit Mme. Khokhlakova (main plot) motivate his recounting to her, in turn, what he knows concerning Dmitry (reconstruction), in explanation of his late night call; his version is then necessarily followed by Mme. Khokhlakova's refutation of the idea that she had ever loaned Dmitry a sum of money (reconstruction); the whole business is then concluded by Perkhotin's hasty departure (main plot). The progress of the story, on one plane, is thereby interrupted by the various reconstructions on another, which either motivate the further progress of the plot or prompt a subsequent response—in the form of a new recapitulation.

In recapitulating information for the reader, the novelist utilizes several basic types of reconstruction which in turn allow for their employment in various possible combinations. A simple typology (analogous to that in Chapter Four), accounting for three principal forms of reconstruction, may be outlined here. Which type is employed at any given stage of the narrative is determined by the question of how much emphasis, if any, is to be placed on a specific incident or on its peculiar perception.

In the sparest form of reconstruction, pared down to the bare statement of "fact," there is no special emphasis or specifying detail. As the most minimal form, designed only to enumerate a series of events, it allows the story to progress without any considered reflection upon a particular incident, beyond noting its having taken place, as the following examples show.

> And Mitya described how he took the pestle and ran. He told them how he had leaped over the fence into his father's garden; how he had gone up to the window; told them all that had passed under the window. (455)

> (Here the prosecutor described the meeting of the family at the monastery, the conversations with Alesha, and the horrible scene of violence when the defendant had rushed into his father's house just after dinner.) (668)

> Here Ippolit Kirillovich passed to a detailed description of all Mitya's efforts to borrow the money in order to avoid the crime. He described his visit to Samsonov, his journey to Lyagavy, all of which were attested to. (669)

> But he described minutely Mitya's exploits in the Metropolis, all his compromising doings and sayings, and told the story of Captain Snegirev's "wisp of tow." (663)

> (Then followed the anecdote about Captain Snegirev.) (668)

Having already been recounted three times in the novel, the Snegirev incident is not to be repeated again; no further emphasis is placed on it. Similarly, no special attention is given any aspect of the above entirely denuded "accounts."

In the "fragmented" or "truncated" reconstruction, a specific detail is highlighted to the exclusion of others, or a certain reaction on the part of a character is emphasized, generally by the incorporation of direct speech into the narrative flow. To this type belong Fenya's near hysterical assertions regarding Dmitry's bloodstained hands and Dmitry's own (previously cited) account of what occurred under his father's window.

> "And the blood was simply flowing, dripping from him, dripping!" Fenya kept exclaiming. This horrible detail was simply the product of her disordered imagination. . . .

"And when he came back," Fenya added with excitement, "I told him the whole story, and then I began
asking him, 'Why have you got blood on your hands,
Dmitry Fedorovich?' and he answered that that was
human blood, and that he had just killed someone. He
confessed it all to me, and suddenly ran off like a
madman . . . ." (420-21)

Her telling of things illustrates the highlighting effected by the
reconstruction, whereby certain striking features of an episode—
to the exclusion of others—are filtered through an individual
consciousness which may color it, or, as in this instance, completely distort it.

The maximal type of reconstruction involves the entire
recounting of an event. It provides a piece of previously unknown information, or presents a particular construance of an
event, as interpreted by a particular intellect, in great enough
detail for the reader to comprehend the rationale behind the
deed. The case in point is rendered by Smerdyakov at the end.

In the final books of the novel, where the anecdote—contributing essentially new information—gives way as a dominant
form to the reconstruction, which evaluates what for the most
part is already known, the forms just outlined are repeatedly
utilized, generally as a pastiche of all three, in the formation of
past-oriented structures. The entire Book Nine thus follows a
single compositional pattern, with its first two chapters devoted
to reconstructing the events which have led to Dmitry's arrest,
and the remainder, to an account of the preliminary investigation, whose business it is to delve into the recent past. In result,
essentially the same pattern emerges governing this book as
that previously detailed concerning its first chapter; the main
story line, which intends to move toward the conclusion of the
tale, is interrupted by accounts, which ostensibly take it in the
opposite direction. In doing so, however, new significance
derives from the various (past-oriented) accounts—the testimony of Dmitry and others—which together cast great enough

doubt on his actions and subsequent explanations to warrant his standing trial for the murder of his father. Thus the examination of the past—through the various reconstructions of Book Nine—generates the further events of that book, leading to the trial in Book Twelve.

The Trial.

In the several forms just outlined, the reconstruction is most extensively employed in the final book of the novel, devoted to the trial. There what is already known to the reader is presented in truncated form, while a fuller elaboration, through direct discourse or dialogue, is reserved for what is new or contains an element of surprise. The entire period during which the servant Grigory is on the witness stand, for instance, is conveyed to the reader indirectly as a kind of summation—right up to the moment in the cross-examination when he is quizzed on the contents of the "medicine" rubbed on him, which elicits the fact that he was literally soaked in spirit before retiring that night. Similarly, the compromising revelations concerning the supposedly liberal Rakitin are developed through interlocution as direct discourse (maximal reconstruction), while all that precedes regarding Rakitin's testimony is conveyed indirectly (as a mesh of fragmented and minimal reconstructions). As a single unified structure, his testimony, like Grigory's, is presented as a limited kind of pastiche composed of the three basic types of reconstruction. In this sense, it models the composition of all related structures (including all the other witnesses' testimonies) contained in the novel. The overall pattern by which the defense lawyer's feats of disarmament are conveyed to the reader emerges, then, as follows: what is already known is presented in truncated form, at times laced with key phrases directly quoted, leading up to the moment of triumph when the unknown fact is detailed within the framework of the cross-examination as direct discourse bearing new information.

After the testimonies of the various witnesses are either detailed or passed over as offering essentially nothing new, the prosecutor summarizes his case by interpreting events of which the reader is already aware through their initial presentation and later reiteration at the trial. Drawing heavily on a mass of psychological detail, he painstakingly reconstructs what, in essence, never happened. What did, however, turns up in his interpretation of events only in a subordinate clause as a totally unlikely possibility (". . . for Smerdyakov could only have committed the murder after [Dmitry] had knocked Grigory down and run away" 684). By paying careful, precise attention to detail, he reconstructs every possible variant of the night's events, taking each to its logical but incorrect conclusion, as the novel makes its point that logic and human psychology are often at variance. The prosecutor's method, beginning with an "historical survey," entails the systematic reconstruction of what was known to have occurred, followed by reconstructions of a more speculative nature regarding the various possibilities of what could have occurred. From the basic supposition that Dmitry is indeed guilty of his father's murder, all possibilities are examined with their various ramifications duly asserted— and these, fomenting a whole new series of reconstructions, return the prosecutor to his original position, as the labyrinth of his psychology takes him full circle.

In contrast to the prosecutor, who, in formulating his charges, reconstructs the supposed chain of events leading up to the murder by incorporating the evidence submitted by witnesses, the defense lawyer launches his defense for the most part by recapitulating only the basic argument of the prosecutor. But by relying on his governing notion that psychology "cuts both ways," he manages to draw opposite inferences. The arguments of the defense are thus not directed towards reconstructing new possibilities, but are aimed primarily at destroying the constructs of guilt erected by the prosecutor. Throughout, the lawyer's strategy is uniform: to discredit the witnesses, the supposed evidence, and the "psychology" brought to bear against the accused. Hence the prosecutor's reconstructions are themselves reconstructed by a presumably sharp Petersburg lawyer, who contents himself with recreating them "from the other end of the stick," in an attempt to discredit the other's conclusions. But he also blithely misses the point that they are dealing with a case of premeditated murder.

In spite of the conscientious efforts made at the preliminary investigation and trial to reconstruct the chain of events of the one single night, the knowledge of what had really occurred remains within the exclusive province of Smerdyakov alone. Only when the bright, crisp hundred-ruble notes are shown to Ivan does he find himself compelled to acknowledge his former lackey as the murderer of his father. The return of the money signifies the extinguishing of an idea, which had taken monstrous shape in the mind of a lackey with criminal intent and materialist ambitions. Having been shown the money, Ivan must now hear it all out, requiring from Smerdyakov what he had wished all along to avoid: "Only tell me in detail how you did it. Everything, as it happened. Don't forget anything. The details, above everything, the details, I beg you" (592). Smerdyakov's subsequent reconstruction of the crime (running some five pages) is, necessarily, the longest in the novel, since it reconstructs, for the first time accurately, the novel's pivotal event.

*

The murder of Fedor Pavlovich is indisputably the central fact of the novel. All of the events prior to its occurrence lead up to it; all that takes place thereafter focuses back upon it. It has been the thesis of this chapter that the event is pivotal, not only in terms of plot, but compositionally as well. In short, the novel

moves toward the crime with its story developed through a
series of anecdotes, and refers back to that primary event by
means of a series of reconstructions. Through repeated references to a single incident, the anecdote serves to generate the
tale in the first half of the novel. In parallel fashion, the
novelist's technique of returning to an event, reconstructing it,
and viewing it from several perspectives allows for "present"
new meaning to be attached to past episodes, affording the tale
its momentum beyond Book Eight, ultimately taking the novel
to its conclusion. By emphasizing the repeated narration of
anecdotes and later reconstructions of events, our aim has been
to convey—beyond the fact of their basic repetition—a sense of
the novel's ebb and flow, determined by just these governing
structures.

The events of the novel attain a certain dynamic quality
through repeated reference to such episodes as the early meeting between Katerina Ivanovna and Dmitry, the humiliation to
which Dmitry subjects Snegirev, that suffered by Grushenka in
her relationship with the Pole, Dmitry's search for finances
followed by the search for Grushenka, his impulsive seizure of
the murder instrument before the horrified eyes of the maid
servant. All of these events and others have the same resonant
quality—as does the cry at night of "parricide," uttered by
Grigory at the moment he is felled, echoing the future victim's
initial outcry in the cell, and anticipating its being heard once
again in the courtroom. The events themselves and the crucial
phrases connected with them—"I am a scoundrel, but not a
thief"; "I will kill father if only Ivan will leave"; "One serpent
will devour the other"; "The right to my wishes I leave for
myself"—all attain a level of significance which goes beyond
that of their initial depiction or utterance, by virtue of their
very repetition by different personalities offering their unique
individual interpretations in a variety of contexts, ranging from
the intimate meetings between the brothers to such public
occurrences as the investigation and trial. Such "echoes" of the

various incidents and episodes of the novel lend them their dynamic quality of resonance, making of them events which demand, as it were, resurrection. And this is achieved in large measure by the two past-oriented structures here considered.

What these two forms—the anecdote, which eventually gives precedence to the reconstruction as a principal structural element—have in common is the crucial role of linking past to future at the moment of narration. In doing so, both forms may be viewed as dual-directed signs, whose main function is to take the story from its beginning to the novel's end. Within the context of their dual-directed nature, the same holds true for both the anecdote and reconstruction: each conveys certain (past-oriented) information while going beyond that communication to anticipate or generate (as future-oriented) what is yet to come. They each possess a certain regressive relevance by casting new light on an event already described but bear progressive significance as well by virtue of the inherent manner employed in propelling the story of the novel forward. Both structures are thus seen to form part of the novel's linkage system by which the various themes are connected and the story is told. In both there is the very real incorporation of the past into the present—but a present which is itself permeated with a future orientation.

7

Summation

Temporal Strategies

The task of the preceding chapter has been to demonstrate in critical practice a theoretical view concerning *The Brothers* that is expressed by a Russian critic in these terms: "Thus, present and past in the novel are linked with that of becoming, the story about what is and what had been is connected with that of future possibilities, so that it appears at one and the same time as both an analysis of the past and present, and as a projection of the future" (Vetlovskaya 1971:199). Specifically referring to *The Brothers*, that concrete remark bears generally on a more theoretical analogue, whose concern is to point up the governance in narrative of both a "principle of succession" as well as a "principle of simultaneity." As a representative instance of such analogue, the idea is explained by an American theorist thus: "The artistic text is . . . marked not only by an anticipatory development, but also by a retroactive impulse which integrates the elements of succession" (Stankiewicz 1974:643). Expanding upon this notion, the Czech thinker, Jan Mukařovský, explains: "On account of reciprocity, motivation has at the same time a progressive and regressive character. When the initial member of a motivational bond appears, it evokes an expectation in the perceiver; the next then directs the perceiver's attention backwards to what has already been perceived" (1977:198-99). In other words—and this, in effect, defines our project here—the

critic must take into account "the forward and backward movement of the text along the syntagmatic axis" (Stankiewicz
1977:70), as projected in novelistic time. Having assailed that
task critically in the preceding chapter, we will now return to
it briefly in its more general, theoretical aspect.

For two of the most important literary theorists of this
century, Georg Lukács and Mikhail Bakhtin, the epic—as opposed to the novel—represents the genre that most clearly
reflects a given order to the world. The epic depicts a world
which is ordered and finished; its hero's role is predetermined
by his place in that world. The novel reveals a private and public
sphere which is contingent and indeterminate; its hero attempts to give meaning to life in spite of the oppressive uncertainty and indeterminacy. As Lukács puts it: "The novel is the
epic of an age in which the extensive totality of life is no longer
given, in which the immanence of meaning in life has become
a problem, yet which still thinks in terms of totality . . . .the
novel seeks, by giving form, to uncover the concealed totality of
life" (1971:56,60). This effort to reveal a "concealed totality" is
achieved in large part through the novelist's utilization of time
as a crucial determining factor. Where the novel attempts to
reflect an ordered world, or one seemingly capable of being
organized and ordered, according to certain basic precepts,
time, as a principal constituent element of the novel, is itself
arranged and ordered according to certain fundamental patterns, which afford the sense of that totality.

In the jointly held view of Lukács and Bakhtin, time defines
the genre of the novel in opposition to the timeless quality of
the epic. But time is a crucial aspect of all narrative; in fact, no
narrative structure can proceed to unfold without recourse to
temporal considerations. As the Soviet semiotician, V.V. Ivanov,
puts it: time is "a category outside of which the artist's intention cannot be realized" (1973:1). Central importance is similarly ascribed to the novel's temporal considerations by numerous
others. Thus, "In the final analysis, virtually all the techniques

and devices of fiction reduce themselves to the treatment accorded to the different time-values and time-series, and to the
way one is played off against another" (A.A. Mendilow 1952:63).
In principle, that assertion corresponds to Bakhtin's conception
of the novel "as an image of temporal art; one that represents
spatially perceptible phenomena in their movement and development" (1981:251). That general view notwithstanding, with
regard to the Dostoevsky novel in particular, Bakhtin accords
spatial concerns primacy, when he remarks that the Russian
novelist "conceived his world primarily in terms of space, not
time" (1984:28). Primacy here, in any case, in the form of the
last word to a question that will not be immediately resolved, is
accorded E.M. Forster, who assures us that time is "far more
fatal than place" (1927:29).

That "fatal" concern, constituting an immense topic by
anyone's standards, will be radically consolidated, in these concluding remarks, to the relation of time and ideology from the
delimited perspective of the Dostoevsky novel. This special,
unique corpus—quintessentially representative, in at least this
one respect, of the traditional nineteenth-century novel in
general—is defined by that metaphysical search for what
Lukács deems (in relation to the timelessness of the epic) a lost
totality. Such orientation, however, necessarily implies a corresponding belief that the world itself, as reflected in the novel,
is similarly subject to some principle of organization. One level
on which this "search" is clearly realized within the aesthetic
confines of the novel is the temporal, with time organized in
such a way as to suggest that the world of the novel—as
analogous hypothetical construct to the world it models—is
indeed governed by a certain meaningful order. This fundamentally positive viewpoint, constituting a kind of faith,[1] informs
an entire body of fictional narrative with a sense of uniformity
by virtue of its attempting to effect a thematic resolution in a
way perhaps more difficult to discern in much of twentieth-
century narrative. There meaning has become peripheral and

ephemeral, marked more by the chaos envisioned by Dostoevsky than by the order sought by Tolstoy's heroes intent upon
giving meaning to their lives and their world. "Prophet" of
chaos, according to certain popular acclaim, Dostoevsky nevertheless has likewise created a world founded on a principle of
continuity and order, reflected in a logically ordered temporal
framework.

Briefly considered, that order may be approached from two
linked perspectives. First, the least complex narrative from a
temporal standpoint constitutes a series of episodes presented
in linear chronological sequence. Sequential order and caus-
ality, however, do not necessarily coincide. A narrative's chain
of events may simply follow one another, or they may stand as
well in more complex, *causal* relation to each other.[2] In this
latter case, a text (or part of one) may therefore yield a set of
relations that are not only sequential but generative as well,
with one episode clearly motivating the next. Time, in either
case, however, ultimately reduces to essentially the same linear
pattern as in life—but with a single, crucial difference: the
conventional work of fiction, by contrast, requires some form of
motivation to make its sequence of events comprehensible and
credible. The Formalist theorist, Boris Tomashevsky, argues
therefore that an underlying rationale or motivating factor
(*motivirovka*) in the literary work is an essential plot component (1928:144-52). Aside from being subject to the governance of a certain temporal order, in other words, the series of
events composing the narrative must be clearly motivated in
order that the plot be generated; a more or less believable
rationale for what has already occurred is the prerequisite for
what follows. Logical causal relations between past, present,
and future are therefore retained. Conventional in this respect,
the architectonics of Dostoevsky's novels conform to this basic
constraint, resulting in a certain meaning or truth being inex-
tricably bound to the moment at which it is revealed.

All narrative is ordered at least in part according to a linear chronological sequence. Each component sequence is structured, moreover, in the form of a series of indexical signs that are both single-directed and future-oriented, designed to take the plot forward, in relatively direct fashion, to its eventual resolution.[3] By contrast, when a text is not ordered according to a straightforward, linear progression but follows instead an inverted chronological system, it allows for references to both past and future events to be incorporated within its overall temporal framework, characterized by a reconsideration of the past (offering regressive relevance) coupled with references to the future (providing progressive significance). Thus, as Mukařovský points out: "There is always something in the work which is bound to the past and something which points to the future" (1970:35).

In the simpler, linear sequential ordering of events, the movement of the plot proceeds through a series of single-directed (future-oriented) indexical signs; in the more complex inverted chronological structure, the plot develops by means of a series of dual-directed indices, determined by their dual temporal orientation. When a past-oriented account—created by a certain temporal disjuncture (as the plot regresses from present to past, affording a retrospective view)—emerges as central, it must nevertheless be taken as future-directed as well, since it refers to the past largely to make comprehensible what is yet to occur in the future. Its ostensible past orientation, in other words, is only the more evident aspect of its corresponding future directedness. Serving as a work's connective linkage, however, both indexical forms provide a rationale for additional episodes by revealing further linkages between what has been dramatized for the reader and what has not. From the standpoint of time, the index is thus at once the principal sign and substance of verbal art, pointing, on the one hand, to what is either past or future, while itself serving as the object of representation, which, at any given moment, is always present.[4]

Within these two interlocking temporal structures, with one continuously embedded within the other, the respective ideational plans of Dostoevsky's novels are realized. In both *Crime and Punishment* and *The Idiot*, the stories unfold essentially in chronological order. There are few fully developed retrospective references. Myshkin's account of his life in Switzerland, as an exception, represents one such instance. In *The Possessed* and *The Brothers*, by contrast, the chronological arrangement of events is more complex. The past in each of the later novels plays a greater role in what unfolds in the present. Yet whether that unfolding—in relatively straightforward or more complex temporal arrangement—affords in any of the works a clear, positive resolution to plots encompassing, respectively, Raskolnikov's seeming repentance, Myshkin's madness, Stavrogin's suicide, or the children's ambiguous celebration of the Karamazov spirit, remains problematic at least—and a source of further readings.

One critic concerned with the problem of time in narrative speaks of there being "an acute consciousness on the part of writers that literature is a time-art, in which the continuum of the text is apprehended by the reader in a continuum of time and ... that these conditions may be exploited and manipulated in order to produce various effects on the reader" (Sternberg 1978:34). One, perhaps most important, sought-after effect is to give the sense of a world in which the possibility for rational organization and corresponding meaning is not yet lost. Hence, in the traditional novel of resolution, there is the fundamental presupposition that the represented world of the novel is ordered according to a certain pattern or set of (partially) codified principles based on that of the real world it models. "Since authors model whole worlds, they are ineluctably forced to employ the organizing categories of the worlds that they themselves inhabit" (Clark and Holquist 1984:278). Conversely, the actual world may either be ordered according to the way it is modeled in the novel or the possibility of its being so is nevertheless seen to exist. However, if the novel indeed models an ordered, recognizable world, then that depicted world, in turn, reflects the literary form from which it derives, suggesting, first of all, that the novel itself is subject to a related system of organization, of which time considerations are a principal constituent. The traditional novel is thus governed by a consistent system of organization which is delimitable in its temporal confines, and which therefore affords a certain modicum of meaning by virtue of that clearly evident organization.

Regarding such modicum, Lukács observes that "The immanence of meaning which the form of the novel requires lies in the hero's finding out . . . that a mere glimpse of meaning is the highest that life has to offer . . . " (1971:80). Likewise, the reader, it is presumed, can seek no less, nor attain any more. But if that conservative assessment, offered by Lukács, is indeed all we (and the hero) are afforded by the novel, it is attainable, because "In the traditional narrative of resolution, there is a sense of problem solving, of things being worked out in some way, of a kind of ratiocinative or emotional teleology" (Chatman 1978:48). We need only apply, in other words, Barthes' "hermeneutic" code, "by means of which the narrative raises questions, creates suspense and mystery, before resolving these as it proceeds along its course" (Hawkes 1977:116).

But what if that "mystery" encompasses the world itself? As one response, we may say with Bakhtin that "however immutable the presence of that categorical boundary line between [the real and the represented world], they are nevertheless indissolubly tied up with each other and find themselves in mutual interaction . . . " (1981:254). The codes of the one, in other words, determine and are reflected in those of the other, yielding a reciprocal relation that *seeks*, at least, "a mere glimpse of meaning."

Perhaps, as Lukács holds, "the entire inner action of the novel is nothing but a struggle against the power of time" (1971:122), as it is in life. If so, in narrative in general, and as practiced by Dostoevsky like no other, that struggle is characterized by an ever-present endeavor to provide in aesthetic formulation a resolution to the suspense, the plot, the mystery of the novel, and the mystery that is the world.

Notes

Portions of this book have been published in earlier versions that have since been substantially revised. They include: "Semiotics of Gesture in Dostoevskian Dialogue," *Russian Literature*, VIII-I (January 1980), 41-75; "Notes on Generating a Text: *The Brothers Karamazov*," *Modern Language Studies*, XI:1 (Winter 1980-81), 75-95; "Subtexts of *The Brothers Karamazov*," *Russian Literature*, XI-II (February 1982), 173-208; "Dialogic Structures in *Crime and Punishment*," *Russian Literature*, XIX-III (April 1986), 291-314; "Stavrogin's Teachings: Reported Speech in *The Possessed*," *Slavic and East European Journal*, XXXII, 2 (1988), 213-224; "Diegesis in *The Idiot*," *Language and Style*, XXII, 2 (Spring 1989).

Chapter One.

1. Generally precluded from our understanding of "dialogue" in this book are such figurative formulations as those which embrace the concept of "dialogic relationships among texts and within the text" (Bakhtin 1986:105). Rather, our guiding premise is to accord the term its concrete understanding as, what Bakhtin calls, "Real dialogue (daily conversation, scientific discussion, political debate, and so forth)," (Ibid.: 124), whose defining quality is its responsiveness to other communication.
2. For an elaboration of the concept of reported speech used as a means for directing, or influencing, the reception of a given point of view, see Voloshinov's discussion (1973:120-22) of what he terms the *pictorial* mode of speech reporting.

Chapter Two.

1. The term is intended here in the same general sense assigned it by A.A. Ilyushin (1969:22): "gesture is to be understood in the broadest sense as the movement not only of the hands but of the entire body, including facial expression."

2. In this basic reciprocal relationship, gestures "do not so much accompany replies as replace them." Conversely, "the reply . . . becomes in essence a manifestation of that which is already contained in the gesture" (Mikhailov 1972:102).

3. In most instances, the religious figures of the novels are especially gifted in this respect. An exception, Porfiry Petrovich, the detective in *Crime and Punishment*, utilizes and interprets the "language of gesture" with consummmate skill.

4. "The motifs 'I didn't know that,' 'I didn't see that,' 'that was revealed to me only later,' are absent from Dostoevsky's world. His hero knows and sees everything from the very beginning" (Bakhtin 1984:239).

5. Similarly, at Dmitry's trial in *The Brothers*, Alesha declares that he knows his brother is telling the truth simply by looking at him. "I saw from his face he wasn't lying" (643). That remark constitutes his sole proof of his brother's innocence.

6. In this and subsequent instances, where the citation refers to the original Russian text (volume and page), the passage has been omitted from the English translation (as noted in the preface).

7. A Russian sect which practiced self-mutilation.

8. Originally designating the wandering pilgrims who traversed the Russian countryside as a self-imposed religious duty, the term has a long history in the Russian folk tradition. In the present context (and generally in Dostoevsky), it refers to someone who is weak intellectually but has great spiritual insight and understanding. "She has religious mania!" (311), as rendered in the English text, conveys little of the sense of this culturally important term.

Chapter Three.

1. The inner tension of the novel is built on a triadic principle: "The central dynamic of the novel . . . is in the Myshkin-Nastasya-Rogozhin relationship" (Dalton 1979:60). That view, corresponding to the one taken here, implicitly reduces Aglaya's importance to that of the second woman in Myshkin's life, thereby serving as the opposite pole in a secondary field of tension between herself and Nastasya Filippovna, with Myshkin—at a climactic moment—caught irresolutely between them.

2. As A.A. Mendilow observes: "The dramatic method aims at conveying 'the psychological equivalent of the dramatic present.' . . . The lavish use of dialogue is an important element in the dramatic method, and is perhaps the most obvious means of producing the illusion of immediacy and presentness in the reader" (1952:112).

3. Essentially the same distinction is made by Robin Miller (1981), when she notes a shift from the "descriptive mode" to the "dramatic," in discussing narrative point of view in the novel.

4. The irony of the situation is pointed out by Michael Holquist: "Burdovsky seeks to establish the identity of his father in order to gain a part of his inheritance; his problem is that of all the other characters: to discover the identity of his true parents. He differs from the others only in that he succeeds where they fail" (1977:119-20).

5. The concept is further complicated by the fact that Stavrogin is not only "other" to his disciples but distinctly so to his past self as well. While this "dichotomy" (crudely put as the recognition of a clear difference existing between one's past and present ego) corresponds to the thinking of C.S. Peirce, Bakhtin and others, *The Possessed* documents the idea in art.

Chapter Four.

1. This type of report is closely related to Voloshinov's "texture-analyzing modification," where "words and locutions are incorporated in

such a way that their specificity, their subjectivity, their typicality are distinctly felt" (1973:131).

2. Voloshinov assigns three basic templates to the problem of reported speech: direct discourse, indirect discourse, and quasi-direct discourse. The latter exhibits the greatest complexity and corresponding interest. Regarding quasi-direct discourse, Voloshinov notes that "the boundaries of the message are maximally weakened" as "half narration and half reported speech" (1973:122,134). Requiring a determination as to *whose* word is articulated at a given moment, the *"specificum"* of this challenging framework "is precisely a matter of *both* author *and* character speaking at the same time, a matter of a single linguistic construction within which the accents of two differently oriented voices are maintained." Quasi-direct discourse expresses "an active orientation . . . that imposes upon the reported utterance its own accents, which collide and interfere with the accents in the reported utterance . . . .In quasi-direct discourse, we recognize another person's utterance not so much in terms of its message, abstractly considered, but above all in terms of the reported character's accentuation and intonation, in terms of the evaluative orientation of his speech" (Ibid.: 144,154-55).

Hence the two speeches interfere "to the extent that it is impossible to unambiguously determine which is at work in a particular word . . . . The unresolvably problematic character of the text defies the attempt to sum up in a single speech the interplay of speeches within it" (Silverman and Torode 1980:308). That "defiance" points up the basic challenge of this chapter.

Chapter Five.

1. For "The Grand Inquisitor," a more elevated term such as "incorporated novella" would likely be more appropriate. However, the criteria suggested under the chosen, more broadly applicable rubric will accommodate, without qualification, Ivan's expansive "poem."

2. Important parallels to Grushenka's tale are Alesha's vision of Cana of Galilee and Dmitry's dream of the "babe," both of which yield a new vision of the world, in which the spirit guides. All three instances support the commonly held view (e.g., Silbajoris 1963:28; Matlaw 1957:20) that the major metaphor of the novel is resurrection—from doubt (Alesha), from a wasteful profligate existence (Dmitry), from the gnawing past (Grushenka).

3. In addition, the passage anticipates Ivan's collapse as thinker, since his first premise, as related by Miusov, undermines the argument of the Grand Inquisitor, who claims to love man more than Christ. That premise states that, if there were such a thing as love for one's fellow man, it would stem from the belief in one's immortality. Ivan admits to Alesha, however, immediately upon the conclusion of his recitation of "The Grand Inquisitor," that the imperious old man had lost his faith in God (and, consequently, in his own immortality), as Alesha had surmised. Therefore, his rational organization of society for the happiness of the majority is not based on love for mankind as Ivan would have it, but stems from his contemptuous view of man as being incapable of dealing with freedom.

4. There are repeated references in the novel to Kolya's misadventure, which represent intimations of a story yet to be told. These references, the story's "kernels," as it were, appear as follows: (a) "Six weeks later, it is true, [Kolya] got into another scrape, which even brought his name to the ears of our justice of the peace . . . But of this later" (489). (b) "Only don't tease them, please, or you'll get into another scrape as you did about that goose" (499). (c) "What's undermined my reputation more than anything here was that cursed goose" (517). That last reference is made by Kolya himself and serves as the prelude to his finally rendering the account in detail.

5. At the same time we must recognize that the tale (as an independent sign abstracted from the text) is itself composed of a signifier (its form) and signified (what it purports to relate). Yet within the text, and therefore on another plane of meaning, the tale functions as signifier of one of the novel's underlying concepts, which becomes the "new" signified (through critical interpretation)– and which

provides the rationale for the tale's inclusion in the novel in the first place.

6. The juxtaposition of the two works may also be read as supportive of Ivan's overall position of rebellion. In the tale, the Virgin requests that all those in hell be forgiven "without distinction." The tale may thus be viewed as a parallel to "The Grand Inquisitor," since the basic motif is the same. "The Virgin here raises her own 'rebellion' against human suffering, a rebellion against a cruel-hearted God. In this discussion [between God and the Virgin, which Ivan cites], a protest against God's (social) injustice in the world order [*miro-ustrojstvo*] is made evident, a protest which resounds with enormous force in Ivan's own rebellion" (V.V. Kuskov 1971:23).

Chapter Six.

1. That Snegirev opens his heart to Alesha, telling him of his troubles and humiliation, is consistent with other disclosures made by nearly all of the novel's major characters, whose intimate revelations are shared always and only with Alesha. Being the recipient of such information defines to large degree his role in the novel: he is the messenger commissioned to perform a variety of tasks and the trusted confidant of all the dramatis personae. To invoke the Formalist metaphor, Alesha may be likened to the string on which the beads of the story are strung. But such figurative notion takes on concrete dimension when it is recognized that virtually all of the characters of the novel are strangely isolated from one another, although their stories and destinies are interwoven. Thus, Ivan and Dmitry are never depicted exchanging a single word; Dmitry's dialogue with his father is limited to the one verbal encounter in the cell and a single statement of warning and disavowal ("The Sensualists"); Dmitry is never shown conversing with Smerdyakov although the latter repeatedly testifies that he is in mortal fear of him as a result of their encounters offstage; further, Dmitry exchanges only a few words with Katerina Ivanovna at the close of the

novel preceded only by the single outcry to her in the courtroom ("Katya, why have you ruined me?" 647); Ivan never converses with Grushenka; nor she with Fedor Pavlovich, with whom her fate is irrevocably intertwined because of his death (and her passive role in it) and the subsequent verdict rendered against Dmitry. Clearly, then, there must be some link or intermediary among all the principals—and this role is fulfilled by the third, gentle, noncritical and nonjudgmental son of Fedor Pavlovich.

Chapter Seven.

1. That faith is neatly encapsulated in a remark made in *Anna Karenina* by Levin, one of Tolstoy's seekers, concerned to arrange his life according to certain cherished tenets that would extend to "the little circle of our district, then the province, then Russia, then the whole world. Because a just idea cannot but be fruitful" (1970:364). Characterizing a view that may well not have survived into the present century, the latter sentiment may be seen as both aphoristic and indicative of that (lost) faith.

2. As Aristotle affirmed: "It makes a great difference whether . . . events are the result of . . . others or merely follow them" (*Poetics* 1452a21).

3. As Barthes puts it, indices are "integrative elements . . . .bits of *information* used to identify or pinpoint certain elements of time and space" (1974: 246,249).

4. In spatial terms, however, the sign's iconic feature (no sign, after all, is defined by a single function exclusively) appears fundamental to the task of mirroring, in each representative instance, some aspect of the world (the Petersburg Haymarket Square, the Russian provincial town), and allows, ultimately, for the entire text to serve as model of a recognizable world.

   Segre neatly defines the "text" as "a whole made up of signs whose progressively larger groupings . . . serve in their turn as signs" (1979:3). The text is thus composed of "sign complexes" which structure all aspects of the text, itself a highly complex sign. One way by which that complexity is achieved is by virtue of the sign function-ing indexically, in the temporal respect, and iconically, in the spatial terms just noted.

In other, more comprehensive expression, as held by Bakhtin, "Language in the novel not only represents, but itself serves as the object of representation" (1981:49).

Selected Bibliography

Primary Sources.

Dostoevskij, F.M. (1972-). *Polnoe sobranie sočinenij v tridcati tomax*, Vols. 6, 8, 10, 14, 15. Leningrad: Nauka.

Dostoevsky, Fyodor (1976). *The Brothers Karamazov* (Norton Critical Edition), Ralph E. Matlaw (ed.); trans. by Constance Garnett. New York: W.W. Norton.

—— (1964). *Crime and Punishment* (Norton Critical Edition), George Gibian (ed.); trans. by Jessie Coulson. New York: W.W. Norton.

—— (1971). *The Idiot*. Trans. by Constance Garnett. New York: Bantam.

—— (1961). *The Possessed*. Trans. by Constance Garnett. New York: Dell.

Secondary Sources.

Aristotle (1965). *Poetics*. Trans. by W. Fyfe. Cambridge, Mass. and London: Loeb Classical Library.

Bakhtin, M.M. (1981). *The Dialogic Imagination; Four Essays by M.M. Bakhtin*. Michael Holquist (ed.); trans. by Caryl Emerson and Michael Holquist. Austin: University of Texas Press.

—— (1984). *Problems of Dostoevsky's Poetics* (= Theory and History of Literature, Vol.8). Trans. by Caryl Emerson (ed.). Minneapolis: University of Minnesota Press.

—— (1986). *Speech Genres and Other Late Essays* (= University of Texas Press Slavic Series, No.8). Caryl Emerson and Michael Holquist (eds.); trans. by Vern W. McGee. Austin: University of Texas Press.

Barthes, Roland (1974). An introduction to the structural analysis of narrative. *New Literary History*, 6 (2), 237-272.

Belknap, Robert (1968). *The Structure of The Brothers Karamazov*. The Hague: Mouton.

Chatman, Seymour (1978). *Story and Discourse*. Ithaca: Cornell University Press.

Clark, Katerina and Michael Holquist (1984). *Mikhail Bakhtin*. Cambridge: Harvard University Press.

Culler, Jonathan (1975). *Structuralist Poetics; Structuralism, Linguistics, and the Study of Literature*. Ithaca: Cornell University Press.

Dalton, Elizabeth (1979). *Unconscious Structure in The Idiot: A Study in Literature and Psychoanalysis*. Princeton: Princeton University Press.

Danow, David K. (1986). Temporal strategies and constraints in narrative. *Semiotica* 58–3/4, 245-268.

—— (1987). Literary Models and the Study of Narrative. *American Journal of Semiotics* V, 3/4, 461-477.

—— (1991). *The Thought of Mikhail Bakhtin: From Word to Culture*. New York: St. Martin's Press.

Forster, E.M. (1927). *Aspects of the Novel*. New York: Harcourt, Brace and World.

Genette, Gerard (1980). *Narrative Discourse; An Essay in Method*. Trans. by Jane E. Lewin. Ithaca: Cornell University Press.

Goldstein, Martin (1970). The debate in *The Brothers Karamazov*. *Slavic and East European Journal*, XIV, 3, 326-340.

Hawkes, Terrence (1977). *Structuralism and Semiotics*. Berkeley and Los Angeles. University of California Press.

Holquist, Michael (1977). *Dostoevsky and the Novel*. Princeton: Princeton University Press.

Hrushovsky, Benjamin (1976). Poetics, criticism, science; remarks on the fields and responsibilities of the study of literature. *PTL: A Journal for Descriptive Poetics and Theory of Literature*, I (1), iii-xxxv.

Ilyušin, A.A. (1969). Glagoly žesta u F.M. Dostoevskogo. *Russkaja rečʹ*, 6.

Ivanov, Viach. Vs. (1973). The category of time. *Semiotica* 8 (1), 1-45.

Jakobson, Roman (1971). Language in relation to other communication systems. In *Selected Writings*, Vol.II, 697-708. The Hague: Mouton.

Jakubinskij, Lev (1923). O dialogičeskoj reči. *Russkaja reč'*, Sbornik statei pod red. L.V. Ščerby, 96-194. Peterburg.

Kuskov, V.V. (1971). Motivy drevnerusskoj literatury v romane F.M. Dostoevskogo. *Vestnik Moskovskogo Universiteta*, 5.

Lotman, Jurij (1977). *The Structure of the Artistic Text* (=Michigan Slavic Contributions, No.7). Ann Arbor: Department of Slavic Languages and Literatures, University of Michigan.

Lotman, Ju.M. and B.A. Uspensky (1984). *The Semiotics of Russian Culture* (=Michigan Slavic Contributions, No.11). Ann Shukman (ed.). Ann Arbor: Michigan Slavic Publications.

Lotman, Ju.M. et al (1975). Theses on the semiotic study of cultures (as applied to Slavic texts). In *The Tell-Tale Sign; A Survey of Semiotics*, Thomas A. Sebeok (ed.), 57-83. Lisse: Peter de Ridder Press.

Lukács, George (1971). *The Theory of the Novel*. Cambridge: M.I.T. Press.

Matlaw, Ralph (1957). *The Brothers Karamazov: Novelistic Technique*. The Hague: Mouton.

Mendilow, A.A. (1952). *Time and the Novel*. New York: Humanities Press.

Meyerhoff, Hans (1955). *Time in Literature*. Berkeley and Los Angeles: University of California Press.

Mixailov, M.I. (1972). K probleme sjužetno-kompozicionnoj realizacii slova v 'Brat'jax Karamazovyx' F.M. Dostoevskogo. *Učenie zapiski*, vyp. 132, 102-105. Gor'kij: Gor'kovskij Gosudarstvennyj Universitet imeni N.I. Lobačevskogo.

Miller, Robin (1981). *Dostoevsky and The Idiot; Author, Narrator, and Reader*. Cambridge: Harvard University Press.

Mochulsky, Konstantin, (1971). *Dostoevsky; His Life and Art*. Princeton: Princeton University Press.

Morson, Gary Saul (1978). The heresiarch of *META*. *PTL: A Journal for Descriptive Poetics and Theory of Literature*, 3, 407-427.

——(1978). Verbal Pollution in *The Brothers Karamazov*. *PTL: A Journal for Descriptive Poetics and Theory of Literature*, 3, 223-233.

Mukařovský, Jan (1970). *Aesthetic Function, Norm and Value as Social Facts* (=Michigan Slavic Contributions, No.3). Trans. by Mark E. Suino.

—— (1977). *The Word and Verbal Art; Selected Essays by Jan Mukařovský.* Trans. by John Burbank and Peter Steiner (eds.). New Haven and London: Yale University Press.

—— (1978). *Structure, Sign, and Function; Selected Essays by Jan Mukařovský.* Trans. by John Burbank and Peter Steiner (eds.). New Haven and London: Yale University Press.

O'Toole, L. Michael (1982). *Structure, Style and Interpretation in the Russian Short Story.* New Haven: Yale University Press.

Rimmon-Kenan, Shlomith (1983). *Narrative Fiction: Contemporary Poetics.* London and New York: Methuen.

Sebeok, Thomas A. (1976). *Contributions to the Doctrine of Signs* (=Studies in Semiotics, Vol.5). Bloomington: Indiana University Press.

Sebeok, Thomas A. (ed.), (1975). *The Tell-Tale Sign.* Lisse: The Peter de Ridder Press.

—— (1977). A Perfusion of Signs. Bloomington: Indiana University Press.

Segre, Cesare (1979). *Structures and Time.* Chicago: University of Chicago Press.

Shukman, Ann (1976). *Literature and Semiotics: A Study of the Writings of Yu.M. Lotman.* Amsterdam: North Holland Press.

Silbajoris, Rimvydas (1963). The children in *The Brothers Karamazov. Slavic and East European Journal,* VII, 1, 26-38.

Silverman, David and Brian Torode (1980). *The Material Word; Some Theories of Language and Its Limits* (London and Boston).

Stankiewicz, Edward (1974). Structural poetics and linguistics. In *Linguistics and Adjacent Arts and Sciences* (=Current Trends in Linguistics Series), Thomas A. Sebeok (ed.), Vol.12, 629-659. The Hague: Mouton.

—— (1977). Poetics and verbal art. In *A Perfusion of Signs,* Thomas A. Sebeok (ed.), 54-76. Bloomington: Indiana University Press.

Sternberg, Meir (1978). *Expositional Modes and Temporal Ordering in Fiction.* Baltimore: Johns Hopkins University Press.

Stolz, Benjamin A., I.R. Titunik, and Lubomír Doležel (eds.), (1984). *Language and Literary Theory* (=Papers in Slavic Philology, No.5). Ann Arbor: Michigan Slavic Publications.

Terras, Victor (1981). *A Karamazov Companion; Commentary on the Genesis, Language, and Style of Dostoevsky's Novel*. Madison: University of Wisconsin Press.

Todorov, Tzvetan (1977). *The Poetics of Prose*. Trans. by Richard Howard. Ithaca: Cornell University Press.

—— (1981). *Introduction to Poetics* (=Theory and History of Literature, Vol.1). Introduction by Peter Brooks; trans. by Richard Howard. Minneapolis: University of Minnesota Press.

Tolstoy, Leo (1965). *Anna Karenina*. Leonard J. Kent and Nina Berberova (eds.); trans. by Constance Garnett. New York: The Modern Library.

Tomaševskij, Boris (1928). *Teorija literatury; poetika*. Ann Arbor: Ardis.

Uspensky, Boris (1973). *A Poetics of Composition; The Structure of the Artistic Text and Typology of a Compositional Form*. Trans. by Valentina Zavarin and Susan Wittig. Berkeley and Los Angeles: University of California Press.

Vetlovskaja, V.E. (1971). Razvjazka v 'Brat'jax Karamazovyx'. In *Poetika i stilistika literatury*. Leningrad.

Vološinov, V.N. (1973). *Marxism and the Philosophy of Language*. Trans. by Ladislav Matejka and I.R. Titunik. New York and London: Seminar Press.

—— (1976). Discourse in life and discourse in art (concerning sociological poetics). In *Freudianism: A Marxist Critique*, trans. by I.R. Titunik and edited with Neal H. Bruss, 93-116. New York: Academic Press.

Winner, Irene and Thomas (1976). The semiotics of cultural texts. *Semiotica* 18:2, 101-156.

MIDDLEBURY STUDIES IN RUSSIAN LANGUAGE AND LITERATURE seeks to expand our knowledge of the latest developments in linguistics, literary and pedagogical scholarship devoted to Russian language and literature. The series includes analyses of texts and authors, translations of significant literary and scholarly works, and writings on theoretical and applied linguistics with special attention to new methods for the teaching of Russian language and literature. The series editor is:

Thomas R. Beyer, Jr.
The Language Schools
Middlebury College
Middlebury, VT 05753

p. 22-29
p. 69-85